WAYS TO GO EAST
FROM KINNEKULLE TO KATHMANDU

ISBN 978-9-16-398194-4

Copyright © 2018 by Ivan Milles

Cover art and vignettes by Nina Lindgren
studiolindgren.com

All rights reserved.

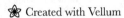 Created with Vellum

Has the journey been worth it? Has the result repaid one for the cold, dirt and privation of Persia, the torrid heat and long desert marches through Baluchistán? Perhaps not.

There are some pleasant hours, however, to look back upon.

— A Ride to India across Persia and Baluchistán,
Harry de Windt (1891)

YOUTUBE

The Radcliffe Line runs from Kashmir down through Rajasthan. If it were a physical line, I would see it from here, snaking through the low grass along a chain-link fence that appears from out of the haze, and joining the brick wall that marks the eastern end of Pakistan. The pale yellow sunset reflects in a golden ornament by the gate into India. Patriotic electro-pop screeches from cracked loudspeakers. "I CAN'T BELIEVE I'M HERE," I yell over the music. My guide nods politely. It is time to take our seats.

Routine can derail into unexpected chains of events. Repeating the same events over and over can build a sort of tension, until the needle hops out of its groove onto an unpredictable path. Routine can wind the springs of an exotic clockwork.

Sunday brunches were one such routine of university life; a way to cap the week and reload for the next. We lived in a student housing complex, all lodgings modelled in the same way: an L-shaped corridor with 10-15 single rooms and a shared kitchen where one of us would invite the others to scones, tea, worn couches and small talk.

The brunches do not come often anymore, but occasionally we gather to see how these adult lives work out, wish for another day of weekend and another teapot.

On one bitterly cold Sunday in February at the end of our studies, a few of us lay defeated in a grey couch, surfing from weird YouTube video to weird YouTube video, and one of those clips stayed with me for years.

It was a military ceremony of some sort. Turban-wearing soldiers in black or khaki and with impressive peacock fans on their heads worked through the moves of an aggressive dance formation. High steps! flags! angry standoffs! flamboyant moustaches! All with a sense of rhythm and ritual. An aggressive but brief handshake, a wrought-iron metal gate clanging shut, two flags being folded up and whisked off into a brick building.

We could not make sense of it. Instead, we giggled and hopped to our feet like children to imitate the stepping, the stomping, the millisecond handshake and the snappy salute. What *is* this? Look it up! Look it up!

It was the evening ceremony of closing the single border station on the Radcliffe line between Pakistan and India.

"We have to go. I have to see this."

PART I

OLD EUROPA

Woke up on a mattress in what used to be my (now empty) room, said goodbye to flatmates, and plodded out in the morning blizzard. Coffee with Dad at the station.

First stop: Mum's house for final preparations: repack the bag five times, print hard copies of travel documents, and then repack the bag again. Birthday dinner for Uncle. Say goodbye to the dogs. Then there are no more excuses. I am going overland, trains and buses to Nepal. I will be away for months and I am going to see that border ceremony along the way.

Mum drives me to the train in Skövde. Wisps of snow across the road in the dark. Arrive, check timetable. Coffee.

Five minutes to departure.

Three minutes.

Backpack. Platform. See you around Easter then, Mum. Bye.

1
ICE38, WITH EXTRA ICE
STOCKHOLM, SWEDEN TO BERLIN, GERMANY

There is a two-hour connection in Katrineholm before the sleeper train to Malmö comes in, but I am much too restless to sit on a bench for two hours. Walk dark and silent streets in snow to find a place to grab a cup of tea but there is nothing open here on Sunday night. The path leads off into a thicket of trees at the edge of town. Tendrils of snow snake across the street here, too.

At this humble beginning, it is hard to tell whether the road will actually take me all the way to Kathmandu from here.

An open pizza place. It is just a fast food place, but tonight it is along the way to the Himalayas. The air shimmers with tension and opportunity. To start softly, a departure entirely without ritual, security check, boarding call or gate. To see the lights on the locomotive behind the bend, the arrival of a train.

After the train pulls into the station, every step on this long journey is my own. I do not know which step is the first. Is the first step the one when I board the train? Or has the first step already been taken?

In my mind's eye, I can see Berlin. I can imagine a train-station in Budapest and I have a hazy idea of what Istanbul will be. But beyond that? A glimmer of Tehran in the corner of my eye. Iran and India separated by an unstable Pakistan. What about the

Himalayas? Kathmandu? Places I only know from childhood Tintin albums. And how will I get back home?

I have stared down my Pakistani visa, trying to figure out whether I should attempt crossing the volatile region of Baluchistan in western Pakistan. I have spent the last six months monitoring that long desert stretch and its capital, Quetta. News, documentaries, travelogues, forum posts, more news. A three-day jeep ride with mandatory escort. Been denied travel insurance for that region everywhere. Baluchistan: 700 kilometres of possible roadblock. Now, exactly how unreasonable is it that the only other person waiting in the station house is an Afghani man who went to school in Quetta?

Now the train's headlights come out of the dark. The rails hiss. A canned voice announces something. There is a flutter in my pulse, but not the faint dread of a runway take-off. This flutter is a time-limited offer to step aboard and come along.

A few hours later, but long before dawn: breakfast in Copenhagen with an American business student producing a travel documentary on his train trip down from Siberia to Munich.

WHEN I GREW up in the mid-eighties and early nineties, the Öresund bridge between Sweden and Denmark had not been built yet. The route to Europe started aboard the Helsingborg-Helsingør ferry, followed by a short drive down through Denmark and the Rødby-Puttgarten ferry. I don't think I have been to Denmark since. It is weird to be back. For a couple of hours, station names are called out in Danish over crackling speakers, and the language's lack of hard consonants still means the same thing as when I was a kid: the Adventure starts here.

Rolling south through Denmark on the Inter-City Express *ICE38* train. We disembark the train on the bottom deck of a ferry and go upstairs. The crossing of the Fehmarn Belt over to Germany is surprisingly windy and rocky today. In Hamburg, my Copenhagen company disappears into the crowds at the Bahnhof. The train stretches out on a non-stop route across the Pomeranian plain. Bleak January light clears up, washing out the bluish-brown murk of dawn, but there is nothing to see outside. A few cows, black trees, dark earth, tilting houses rail-side. Three Danish boys across the aisle wind down from glucose-fuelled play. Villages, fields, rusting evidence of industry.

Suddenly: Spandau station, Zoologischer Garten, Berlin Hauptbahnhof. The city is a lot less inviting than last time. Weather forecast: $-1°C$ + light drizzle = a thin crust of ice over everything. Overcast with a 50% chance of slip-and-fall fracture in the afternoon. I skate down the almost deserted Friedrichstraße into east Berlin. Checkpoint Charlie checked, but it is cold, rainy, raw. The lure of a cosy and warm bed on a south-bound night train is too strong. I skate back up towards the Hauptbahnhof, several icy city blocks at a time, weaving between sparse patches of salt and sand.

From the Hauptbahnhof station, there is a convenient overnight train from Berlin to Budapest. Rail travellers are delivered to Budapest early in the morning, well-rested after a good night's train sleep, right? Ready to go sightseeing and all that, right? Only if you get a bed on the train. You do not get a bed if the train leaves in 30 minutes, and you spend half of them trying to remember where the luggage locker with all your worldly belongings is, and then stand in line for five German-ly effective minutes, and then try to explain that, yes please, I would love a reservation for the train that leaves in ten minutes, *very bitte please*. If you reserve your spot on the night-train with a few hundred seconds to go, you get a coach seat. That chair is opposite a lady in a turquoise jumpsuit who yells at people to be silent all night. You will also be woken up for ticket checks all night: Germany, Czech Republic, Slovakia and Hungary.

You arrive in Budapest with a terrible pain in the neck, funny hair and only automated PriceInfo text messages to tell you where you have been and what it costs to phone home from there.

2
OVERNIGHT ARRANGEMENTS
BUDAPEST, HUNGARY TO SIGHIȘOARA, ROMANIA

Budapest is one of the most beautiful cities in the world, but an overcast Tuesday morning in January through bleary eyes is not a good look on anything. The Budapest-Keleti station spills out into a grey construction site, under a grey overpass under a grey sky. The streets are empty. All street signs are inscrutable and dusted with diacritic marks. It is impossible to tell which way is which or where I am. The first sign of familiarity – a Starbuck's – is enough to pull me in for coffee, text in English and wifi to look up a place to stay.

IN 1873, the three cities of Buda, Pest and Óbuda were united into Budapest. City officials were ordered to search-replace: to change Buda, Pest and Óbuda into the new brand, Budapest. As always with a blind "Replace All," something was lost in the process:

> Problems rose when on a letter coming from Óbuda you could read: "The people of Budapest are sending this letter to the people of Budapest to Budapest."
>
> — AFTER ELEMÉR HORVÁTH

Even though I know the exact address to a hostel, it takes fifteen minutes to find the entrance. Only a closer look at the actual door helps: a small brass plate engraved FRIENDS HOSTEL CALL 22. After a needlessly semantic discussion on the meaning of "available room" I curl up on a simple bed to win back sleep lost on the 477 train between Berlin Hbf. and Budapest-Keleti station.

Late breakfast at Centrál Kávéház with dorm roommate Dimitri, who works in the Russian luxury tourism business. "They will pay anything as long as they feel they get a good deal," he explains. Dimitri has looked up every single restaurant, hotel and attraction in the region and functions as a personal review backing track.

The rail goes east from here and I am not staying. The following afternoon I hold a train ticket into the Carpathians. An oversized burger for dinner – a loaf of bread bisected by a minute steak – and I walk it off pacing up and down the platforms at Keleti station. Trains arrive and leave. Destinations are called out in Hungarian, and reverb between marble floor and vaulted ceiling. This, exactly this evening, this evening spent waiting for a train in a sand-coloured station where the rails run due east, this evening spent waiting for a train to roll out the open end of the departure hall, spent going somewhere, somewhere I cannot really picture yet. This is exactly what I have hoped for.

AN AUSTRALIAN BACKPACKER hunkers into the same train compartment as I, sharing a similar, blurry plan of "Transylvania or something". Together we roll off deeper through the Carpathian basin, and into Romanian night.

3

ASIDE: COUCHETTE CARS

Couchette cars are train compartments that go all *Mickey's Trailer* around midnight. This shelf here turns into a bed and this seat here also turns into a bed and every padded surface in the compartment eventually turns into a bed.

What to expect from top-bunk, mid-bunk and bottom-bunk beds on a typical eastern-European night train:

Top bunk: tricky to get in and out of, but above and away from the other passengers coming in and out of the cabin. No interaction with passengers' midnight bathroom visits, and no people stepping in your face while climbing into their bunks. In fact, you may do the face-stepping. A secure railing saves you from falling out of bed.

Bottom bunk: sleep in the chaos by the door, and your bed is the first stair-step to the upper bunks; but you get a clear view out the window, safe from falling to your death in the middle of the night, and no problems getting in and out of bed and/or the compartment.

Mid-bunk: you claw your fingers into anything – anything – to keep from falling out every time the train brakes, because braking makes your drowsy body roll towards the edge of your 55cm wide excuse for a bunk. No railing.

4
ENTER TRANSYLVANIA
SIGHIŞOARA, ROMANIA

I have been awake for more than an hour when the porter slides open the compartment door, pokes me in the side, whispers "Sighişoara, yes?" and hands my ticket back. Over the hills on the south side of the train, dawn brightens to a wet and overcast morning.

It is not without a certain sense of *what the actual hell am I doing here* I walk along the platform as the train rattles away. No-one in sight. Not sure where I'm going. All I have is a phone screenshot of a map of the general area where there is a hostel.

- Hostel check-in: five hours from now
- Direction: probably somewhere over there
- Distance: probably quite a walk

Before the sun crawls over the forested horizon, the town is a pointy skyline, grey on grey, distances coded in layers of fog. I enter Sighişoara via a cobblestone ramp, through a stone arch under a proper Gothic clock tower with two figurines: Lady Justice and Lady Righteousness, blindfolded and holding a sword, respectively. Except here, in this old fortress, it is Righteousness who is blindfolded, and Justice who holds the sword.

Sighişoara blooms into colour, Bohemian silhouettes and wet cobblestones running off into narrow alleys. Run-down in places, sure, but the turn-of-the-century façades in scarlet, saffron, moss, chalk or rose punch through Transylvanian mist. The mist condenses into a light rain. Wet cobblestones scatter the hues of buildings into a rainbow on granite. Wood-smoke and haze and a clock tower on the summit of the hill beside an ominous church and a brutal ascent along a narrow path. Now a rooster starts crowing but you can go right back to sleep stupid bird because I have been awake since the train passed Daneş and I'm almost at the top and just when I'm cold and tired the hostel has a fire going in the dining hall and my room is just below the slanted tile roof and this is everything I ever hoped Transylvania would be.

Is that a wolf howling? I really, really want it to be, to make the first hour in Draculand complete. It is probably an upset Golden Retriever, but for now, for this moment, it is the Carpathian Beast-Wolf's lonely cry.

One-hundred and seventy-five steps lead from the fortified part of Sighișoara up to *Biserica din Deal*, the Church on the Hill. If the ascent to the fortified town is brutal, this 17th century wooden staircase is the crown jewel. At the top is not only the church, but also the school, where the kids have taken control of the public announcement system. The church guide: "Please do not mind the music. I tell them to turn it down every day, but they turn it back up. I have to be the bad guy, always." Vlad Tepeș himself grew up in the butter-yellow house by the clock tower but descending the winding stairs into this church's crypt is a lot less haunting with Blink 182's *All the Small Things* blaring over the school's loudspeakers above.

As Sighișoara's tourist attractions starts to run out, I am approached by a young tourist guide. After inquiring whether I have any accommodation for the night, he offers a private tour of the older parts of town (all of which are "typical medieval," apparently). Rattling off years and construction dates for every house, tower and street, he leads the way from the typical medieval neighbourhood on down to the lower, 19th century parts of the city.

It is almost dinner time, and the guide offers to recommend a restaurant just down the hill. I need to arrange a train ticket at short notice – the train leaves early tomorrow – and the guide shows me to an ATM just by the restaurant. The sight of me juggling my wallet while trying to keep my nice camera out of the rain is obviously pathetic enough that the guide helps me out.

Wait, wait a minute. A stranger in a leather jacket who claims to be a "tourist guide" now holds my nice camera while I, on this guide's suggestion, withdraws cash from a backstreet ATM in a town that is allegedly the birthplace of Vlad the Impaler, while standing in a night drizzle that makes this look even more like that Eli Roth movie than it already does. A moment of clarity: I know what this looks like. I know how this ends.

(It ends with pizza in the company of Sighișoara's only authorised tour guide at a rosewood-panelled little restaurant).

. . .

IN THE 13TH CENTURY, Andrew II of Hungary invited Saxons from Germany to settle in Transylvania. Founded as one of the seven fortresses of the *Siebenbürgen*, Sighişoara became home for the German settlers. With technology and a skilled workforce, they developed Sighişoara into the centre of a textile proto-industry. Some 700 years later, Romania was clamped between the Soviet and German forces during the war and threw in its lot with the Nazis. When the tide turned, and the Eastern front was pushed back, the Soviet leadership demanded tribute: someone to pay for Romania's alliance with the Germans. Who better, to send to the Soviet labour camps than *ze aktual Germans*? Many generations after they first arrived in Sighişoara, they were shipped off to the Ukraine from the same train station I arrived this morning.

"They said, we will not leave before we hear the church bell from the hill one final time. And the bell was rung once, and then they were gone. We held a memorial service here last week, in fact, with some survivors from that time. We rung the bell once for them, again."

5
KINDNESS OF STRANGERS
BRAȘOV, ROMANIA

You know how they tell you to not look touristy? If you have to look touristy (large backpack, hiking boots, camera), you should not do so right outside the train station. If you have to look touristy, do not look confused and unsure, but try to project certainty. And if you have to do so, do not do it in front of the huge city map on the billboard just outside the station. And if you do, do not attract the attention of strangers.

If you do attract the attention of a stranger, do not answer his "Are you lost, my friend?" with "Yes, I am looking for the tour bus to, um, Dracula's Castle?" And if you do, do not trust the stranger's suggestion to take a taxi to the bus station. And if you do, do not let him hail the taxi for you. And if you do, make sure he does not get in the taxi with you.

But if they do, make sure the driver goes to the place you asked for, and do not accept a more "convenient" destination. But if you do, be a little bit suspicious when they suggest that you take this convenient taxi straight to the "Dracula castle". But even if you are the trusting kind, €25 for a one-hour ride, waiting taxi and return trip should sound the too-good-to-be-true alarm.

But if the alarm doesn't go off, and the taxi does pull up by Castle Bran on time, and the stranger helps you buy the ticket to the castle and then gives you two cell phone numbers to call while he's having coffee with the taxi driver as you bumble around the castle for an hour – if you find yourself in this fairly unlikely situation – don't accept the offer to leave your fucking bag with everything you own in this fucking world in the fucking taxi during that hour.

However, if you do all of the above, you might get a private driver, pizza, a guided tour of Brașov, a ride back to the train station, assistance in buying the train ticket to Bucharest from someone who will wait for the train with you and makes sure you find your seat.

6
200-MINUTE DELAY
BUCHAREST, ROMANIA

The train from Brașov cuts right through the arc of the Carpathian mountains, and then across lowlands covered in more and more snow. Once at Bucharest's Gara de Nord, and after a friend from the train helps me book my next ticket, a small car halts outside the station. Backpack goes into the trunk, his girlfriend waves us in. In freezing rain, she drives through the orange glow of Bucharest's streets, stopping only for traffic lights and reunited couple's kissing across the front seats.

First contact at the hostel: two hungover and jet-lagged Texans who got back from a bar at 6 in the morning, and one of whom finds her clothes hidden in the kitchen icebox. I move into an eight-bed dorm with only a Welsh "humanities something" student for company.

One of the hostel owners takes us to Club Eden, a basement club in the blown-out wine cellar of a 19th century palace. The staircase descending into the vaults evokes *12 Monkeys*, if not the *Saw* movies. But below: a cosy nightclub with a ping-pong table and somewhere to stay out of the snow in good company.

Snow falls all through the night. Bucharest is locked in a blizzard, so I give up my attempt at sightseeing. True to my timetable form, I lose track of time and must hurry through snowdrifts back to the hostel, pull the laundry from a half-finished drying cycle, shovel damp clothes into the backpack, perform an emergency checkout at the front desk, and desperately try to get to the train station in less than half an hour. I zig-zag through streets and squares that look vaguely familiar and across open areas that do not, and miraculously find the train station ten minutes early (getting better!). The train *is* delayed, of course: the signboard says 30 minutes. There is another train marked with a 180-minute delay. Outlook: not so good.

Hundreds of people are waiting for due trains to come down from Carpathia; none arrive. The signboard adds five or ten minutes at a time to the "Delay" column. Maybe the additions will converge on an actual departure, maybe they will not. Snow whirls around us. Travellers drift between the warm waiting hall and the timetable signboard out in the blizzard. My fingers hurt from the cold. Winter-time entrepreneur ladies sell home-knitted sweaters and hats; mulled wine and freshly baked pretzels covered in glittering salt. Wind howls *inside* the half-open departure hall. McDonald's Free Wifi hotspot dies.

The clergy decides to help out. A handsome fellow, wooden sword and cane in hand, aids the spiritual process of freezing to death, to the amusement of many. A TV crew attempts an interview, but the priest is promptly thrown out after he bonks their camera with his sword.

After 200 minutes of patient waiting in the cold, the *Bosphorus Express* appears out of the snowstorm and rolls in to Platform 11. Finally, I can climb aboard into the warm, walnut-panelled compartment, its wooden hues contrasting with the bright-blue cold outside. Heavy blankets tumble out as I unfold the already-made bed. Soft snowflakes, as large as goose-down stick to the window. A ticking radiator warms the compartment and fogs up the glass. My fingers tingle slightly as they thaw out.

Then the conductor informs me that there is a problem with my ticket, asks me to leave the train and try again tomorrow.

THE BLIZZARD IS EVEN WORSE outside the station. Snow reaches up to my knees in places. Pretty sure I am on the right way back to the hostel, but suddenly I am not so sure anymore: lost in a snowstorm on a small, run-down street somewhere by the train station, plodding through snowdrifts and buried sidewalks with an extra-heavy backpack filled with damp or frozen clothes, and my ears might just fall off in the biting cold. There is absolutely no-one around. Alone, tired, cold, possibly lost in a huge city. If I am ever getting into trouble, this is the setting. I will be robbed/stabbed/murdered right here.

And sure enough, there he comes. Prime backstreet stab-murderer talent, yessir! But that is fine, anything to get out of the cold. Stab-murder away all you want, just put me somewhere warm when you are done.

He walks past, and then calls for me once, and then again. Alright, here's trouble. Fists slightly balled. He speaks:

"Don't you have a hat? Do you want mine? It is pretty cold today."

7

WHAT A WONDERFUL WORLD

BUCHAREST, ROMANIA TO ISTANBUL, TURKEY

Today, loudspeakers at the train station play *What a wonderful world*, and the trains' delay column only shows two-digit numbers and McDonald's wifi hotspot is back up and there is almost no wind inside the station and I have a new ticket and the train actually arrives within the hour and *I see trees of green, red roses too…*

I plop down my backpack in the same compartment as yesterday, and I am not getting evicted this time. No sir, my ticket is super-valid and the tricky part at Dimitrovgrad that got me thrown off the train yesterday is doubly covered by both the Interrail pass and a separate ticket into Turkey. But, of course, there is a ticket technicality again. "Maybe problem in Bulgaria," says the purser, "maybe twenty Euro," says the purser, "I ask the Bulgarian staff," says the purser. "That is great," says I, "just super!" I am going to Istanbul either way, "extra charges" or not.

My compartment breathes class and Agatha Christie, the snow stays outside and I am looking forward to eighteen hours of gentle rocking in this little safe-house on rails. Besides, the American father/son duo next door have a bottle of bad wine, served in a green plastic bottle with the neck cut off. Off we go! Cheers!

Oh, that €20 "extra charge"? Can only be paid in cash Euros. No cash Euros? "That's problem," says the purser. We will see.

Might be possible to run to an ATM in Ruse, "if the Bulgarian border police allows it," says the purser. Maybe.

The border police let us out of Romania with a stern knock on the door and a *Passports!* Then comes the Bulgarian side of the border crossing in Ruse. No exiting the train. No ATM. The border police check our passports, eye my visas, ask tough questions: "If you hesitate like that in Iran, no entry!"

The American passports get an extra check to be extra sure. Surly men in puffy jackets with titles embroidered in Cyrillic and with machine guns read out names and passport numbers over crackling walkie-talkies. An authentic experience. While we wait and eat our last food, two train yard technicians decouple a frozen car with a fire-dripping torch. Dinner and a show.

We cross eastern Bulgaria during the night. The little gap between the cabin curtains displays a zoetrope of neon signs, a smattering of street lamps, a pulse of headlights in the landscape outside. The Bulgarian staff comes aboard. I remain unable to produce any Euros for their "extra charge", but the purser hollers down the corridor: "Mister! Ticket is OK! No money!"

Heavy snowfall still. We stop every few hours at small stations, all empty and gloomy, with only skeleton crews to direct us onto the right tracks. We wait while the Turkey-bound half of the Balkan Express from Sofia is spliced onto our Bosphorus Express. No hurry. A soft crackling of snowflakes melting on electric wires overhead. I curl up under blankets in my warm compartment, enjoy the snow and the orange light shimmering in the pearls of ice on my window. The train hums softly in the cold. I would drift off to sleep in a minute if it weren't for the floodlight across the tracks that lights up my compartment like a soccer stadium.

We start moving again. Just before bedtime, the purser gives orders regarding the cabin doors for the night: "Obligation," he yells down the corridor. "Close door, two locks! Two! Two! No close: problem! Close: no problem," he insists. Clear and instructive, if a bit unsettling. What *kind* of problem?

Now it is pitch black outside, apart from snowflakes illuminated by the train. There is a crank to roll down the windows; a smell of snow and wood-smoke from chimneys. Now and then, we pass through villages: houses, dark windows, warm streetlights, vehicles in backyards. We follow snowy roads and cross bridges. On rails, there is scenery out there in the night; something more than just a single red wing-tip lantern.

The compartment is dark, the pillow is fluffy and the snow-show in the dark window is calming... which is why I am pressing my face to the glass and why my pupils are fully dilated when lightning arcs past the glass with a loud boom. Flash-bang. The train hacks to a halt in a tunnel and dies. We are stuck inside a hill, and it takes a long time for a replacement engine to come.

The breakdown delays our Turkish border crossing into the early morning hours. We exit Bulgaria after midnight, and just before 4 in the morning the purser rushes by, knocks the doors and gestures to put on coats and jackets. The fourth passport/visa check for the night takes place in a station house at Turkish Kapıkule, illuminated by naked fluorescent lamps. A dozen shivering tourists purchase visas, get them stamped, visit the decadent tax-free shop.

An Australian backpacker digs out every single coin from his pockets by the visa counter. The price has recently been raised from €30 to €45, and his bills and coins amount to €44. No entry for him. I jog over with a crumpled €5 note and befriend Damon, the cheapest friend I have ever bought.

The fifth visa check of the night comes as a cruel surprise: back in warm compartments, drifting off into a few hours of sleep before Halkalı. *Knock knock!* "Passports!"

At daybreak, there is still snow in the fields to either side of the train. Breakfast: one can of Hungarian knock-off energy drink found in the bottom compartment of my backpack.

HINTS

FOR TRAVELLERS

TO

INDIA, CHINA, & AUSTRALIA.

DETAILING THE SEVERAL ROUTES.

WE ARE ROLLING due east again and India is coming closer with every thud from every passing rail seam under the carriage. India! By train! What an adventure!

During the British Raj, the bank Grindley & Co. (or National Bank of India) anchored the British economy to India. Grindley published a small book: *G. and Co's Overland Circular. Hints for travellers to India*, detailing the several routes available in 1850. Stuffed with advertisements for everything needed when traveling overland from Europe and eastward, it is also a step-by-step manual with timetables, prices, tips and instructions for travellers. A 19th century Lonely Planet guide! What a goldmine!

> Travellers who may wish to visit Constantinople, en route to Alexandria, can proceed by one of the Peninsular and Oriental Company's steamers leaving Southampton on the 27th of every month. These steamers reach Gibraltar in five days, Malta in ten, and Constantinople in about fifteen days from the date of their departure from Southampton.
>
> — G. AND CO'S OVERLAND CIRCULAR (1854)

In summer, an available express route was available: down the Danube, into the Black sea and straight south to Istanbul. "Express route," because "the passage from Vienna to Constantinople is made in *160 hours.*" In that perspective, the last twenty-something hours have been great.

As bleak as the final approach to Halkalı is, it serves as a projection for imagination. Today, the little shrubberies along the highway get to be majestic Thracian olive groves. The Bosphorus

Express train normally terminates in the original, romantic Oriental Express terminus at Sirkeci, but while the Bosphorus tunnel is being constructed it terminates by a roundabout in an Istanbul suburb, where a commuter bus unceremoniously runs the last mile.

In the cold Istanbul morning, we travel partners from the Bosphorus Express look for a hostel. Damon with one Australo-Turkish visa priced at 44+1 euros; Hugh & Aaron having had their American passports scrutinised several times. Superb breakfast kebab off the street at Sirkeci, where the shop owner invites us to his kitchen to roast cold hands over the oven, before Hugh and Aaron head off to their hotel and Damon and I march across the Galatea bridge in search of a hostel marked as a blue pin on a screenshot of a map at a very inconvenient zoom level.

8

MISSING A TRAIN

ISTANBUL, TURKEY TO...

Dear Istanbul, I have been watching you for some time now. I remember you as Constantinople from that weird Disney history album I read when I was eight; the one where Mickey Mouse and Goofy re-enacted Marco Polo? Then, there was that view of the Maiden Tower from the Bond movie – was it The World is not Enough? When we met this white and chilly morning, I found you confusing and a bit distant. But then you warmed my hands on a kebab roaster, and you treated my friends well. I like that.

Damon has raced through Eastern Europe to catch his flight home from Istanbul, cutting it close with only a couple of days to spare. A couple of days is plenty of time to check out from a local hotel and take a taxi to the airport, but being stopped at the border in Bulgaria at midnight is another thing. If he hadn't made it through, I doubt he would have made it back to Sophia or Bucharest in time to fly to Istanbul. But here he is, with a couple of days to spare in one of the greatest cities of the world.

I have a similar problem, though: the *Trans-Asya Express* to Tehran leaves from Ankara... on Wednesdays. Wednesday is tomorrow. The blizzard in Bucharest cut one day from my itinerary, so I must choose between staying one day or staying eight days in Istanbul. Either ferry across the Bosphorus tonight and hop on a night-bus to Ankara, or take what little planning I have and delay it by a full week.

A week is what it took me to get here from my start at Kinnekulle. Stopping and staying in a single city for that many days? Whatever experiences lie ahead will be completely different in a week. On the other hand, racing through Istanbul in an afternoon would be treason to my eight-year-old self.

In the end, Damon cuts the knot for me by suggesting to take the road less travelled. A three-day train to Tehran is definitely a low-flow path, compared to spending a week in Istanbul... but, so far, I have hopped on the next train out as soon as possible: one day here, one day there, one blizzard in Romania. The less travelled road for me would be to stay in one place. We stay idle in the hostel's reception until I have definitely missed the bus to Ankara and then we go out for dinner somewhere.

There are so many trains I have deserved to miss because I showed up just a few minutes before departure. Those lucky near-misses have now been repaid in full: seven days to my account.

∽

DAMON WANTS to set foot in Asia before his long journey is over. We can see the Asian shore from here. It is just a short trip across the Bosphorus strait, so we set early alarm clocks to make the most of his last day. We find a tour that checks off the important parts: the European side, the Bosphorus bridge, the Asian side, and back to Europe in time for lunch. Easy peasy.

The Bosphorus bridge is spectacular from afar and imposing from a-near. It lashes the two halves of sprawling Istanbul together below a white sky. The traffic across it is audible even over the ferry's pounding engine as it cruises along the western, European side of Istanbul's shores, across the strait and back south. But after a long hour on Damon's last day, it is apparent that the tour does not actually *land* on the Anatolian side. The return leg of the tour is just an hour-long tease along docks and jetties on the shoreline while the clock is ticking. Will we have time to spend another hour to find a better tour that will eat up yet another precious hour or two? Tick tock, Damon.

Disappointed back on the pier, we sit down to a rushed fast-food lunch and work the schedule. The correct solution turns out to be a simple commuter ferry across the strait. Fifteen minutes later: problem solved, boots in Anatolia. We trek a long loop up the central hill and then north to look back at the Hagia Sofia from across the Bosphorus. We walk through a quiet residential district, pass by a school, a little mosque, a construction site, and a small grocery store at the top of the hill. Enjoy the crisp winter air.

Adhan, the call to prayer, comes softly here, sudden, close and melodic. One, two, three faithfuls appear from doors and disappear into the mosque's courtyard, one old man still in his slippers.

The sun burns away at the overcast sky. A distinct touch of early spring, a freshness, a warm edge to the cold, a taste of sun that demands a can of Coke because we feel like kids on a school trip again.

9

ALL ROADS LEAD TO THE PUDDING SHOP

ISTANBUL, TURKEY

Our hostel is almost at the top of a long climb up Beyoğlu. Hiking up the hill while cars, mopeds and handcarts freewheel down is rewarded with strong tea in a paper mug from the samovar in the kitchen and a stopover in the couches where new hostel friends intend/pretend to study.

The dorm is on the thousandth floor of a spiral staircase, the bunk bed is welded from aluminium profiles and chicken wire, the shower is always being used by someone else, the railing for the top bunk is missing and the night is cold but blankets are plenty. The view outside: the Galatea tower against the backdrop of mosque domes and minarets over the city's yellow glow and the neon signs in the shopping alley below. The murmur of the night is a lullaby, the sunrise is a gentle start and the hostel is a real home for a few days.

My bunk is pushed up against the wall. On the other side, the 0530 call to prayer is broadcast by a loudspeaker bolted to the side of a minaret. An engineer's guess is an air gap of 3-4 meters, 20-30 cm of brick wall, plaster and a splash of white paint between me and the muezzin's electrically amplified *Come to prayer ... prayer is better than sleep.* After a few days I sleep through it and I worry that I have grown immune to alarm clocks.

The hostel staff take turns at the front desk to play their

favourite music off of YouTube: Passenger, Garfunkel live sets, The Cardigans and Kyuss, and the wifi's leftover bandwidth is throttled to kilobytes/sec. It is raining, but people stream down the hill outside the windows by the hundreds. Another paper mug of tea from the kitchen, and then another one and then we run out for dinner in the rain.

We are, what, five? six? people who hang out in the communal area of the hostel, leaving and coming back in different constellations depending on plans and mood. We go on hours-long walks in Istanbul, trade recommendations, run errands, grab lunch, edit photos and do laundry. We go looking for Michèle's camera battery that was lost in a shop somewhere in Kariköy, visit a mediocre seafood restaurant under Galatea bridge and speculate on why the table behind us left an entire lobster untouched. I go looking for a doctor who can sort out a vaccination I am missing. First down by the harbour where the ferries cross the Bosphorus, and then off İstiklal street, but the hospital lobby is empty and the sun comes out so I put it off and get lost on a warm afternoon in backstreets and alleys with street cats and LED signs and little carts selling bread. We go sightseeing again and have sweet tea in the rain on the steep cliff edge of Gülhane park with a view over the cyan waters of the strait and the beginning of Asia. I can never tire of that view and what it promises.

I walk back to the Sirkeci train station and purchase that one ticket that has the glow of all-caps ADVENTURE: Ankara to Tehran on the Trans-Asya Express. A few tens of Euros for a three-day train journey from Turkey into Iran. I have to go sit down at a quiet café and just look at the ticket's paper envelope, neatly printed with my name in Persian type.

That evening I take another long walk up to a restaurant close to the Blue Mosque and have dinner with Hugh and Aaron from the train and then walk back down in the dark as the bazaar and the market stands pack up and disappear back into little storage areas.

We can go to bed early or late, but the 0530 adhan prayer call is always on time. Prayer is better than sleep, right? Have breakfast and ask the reception if the bed is free for another night because I do not want to leave. It is like the first years of university and I am twenty years old again.

~

"ALL ROADS LEAD TO ROME," – and the original saying "A thousand roads lead to Rome forever" – were probably inspired by the *Milliarium Aureum* (the "golden milestone") in imperial Rome. All roads were said to begin at the milestone, and the distances to all major Roman cities were measured from it – a sort of zero point for the Roman empire. There was also a similar structure for the Byzantine part of the empire: when Constantinople was founded as "New Rome," its *Milion* stone was inscribed with the distances to all major cities of Byzantium. For the past two weeks I have been moving towards the Milion stone, that midpoint of the old empire. I take a detour and make a point of walking past it. It represents the idea that one can reach the same goal by different roads – a traveller's motto. I approach it from the west, pass by it, and start moving east, away from it again.

All of us at the hostel are in transit. Some go home and some keep going further. Damon sneaks out at dawn to Atatürk airport: "Morning, this was fun, see you on Facebook, safe travels!" and he is gone. David moves into a permanent apartment to study. Connor trails a cabin bag out the door and down the hill home to Australia. Sergei is gone one day, Deejay goes the next Monday, Sam in a few days, and then it is my turn to shrug on a backpack and walk up İstiklal to Taksim and roll across the Bosphorus bridge on a night bus.

A stolen week is nearing its end. I will try to miss trains more often.

~

LONELY PLANET, TripAdvisor, The Man in Seat 61, HostelBookers, WikiVoyage, Reddit's */r/travel* and Google Maps are available for the 21st century traveller who wants to go overland from Europe to the East. Back in the 1960's and 1970's, thousands of the Intrepid hippies found roads to travel from Europe to South-East Asia with very little back office support. They blazed the Hippie Trail from London and Copenhagen across the Balkans, Turkey, Syria, Iran, Afghanistan, Pakistan, India and into the kingdom of Nepal, running up in the canonical terminus on the so-called Freak Street in Kathmandu.

Sprawling networks of hitchhikers, buses and Volkswagen Kombis stretched along the routes, with specific hostels, hotels and restaurants acting as hubs for information, planning and connections. Little was written or published; the Hippie Trail was word of mouth.

Istanbul became the first, um, exotic stop on the way from Europe: an intersection for outbound travellers and returning veterans. It all centred on a tiny café near the Blue Mosque.

> The tiny, open-fronted patisserie attracted the attention of the early overlanders, both because of its central location and their sugar-craving munchies. Overnight, the travellers made the Lale their place, renaming it the Pudding Shop ... The well-to-do Turks stood outside, their mouths agape, watching their sons and nephews ... drink coffee with paradise-bound freaks in Apache headbands and paisley waistcoats.
>
> — MAGIC BUS, RORY MACLEAN

The Pudding Shop became the 1960's edition of /r/travel, a central messaging system for the Hippie Trail. The two brothers who owned the Lale Restaurant put up a signboard where overlanders traded tips, looked for travel partners, looked for advice on places to crash in Afghanistan and looked for each other.

I drag friends here to look at a signboard on the wall, though hardly authentic. The aesthetic lives on, but smartphones are a better option today. We can avoid the heartbreak of a note in green ballpoint pen, allegedly written decades ago:

Banjo Lee
Couldn't wait any longer.
Gone to Kathmandu.
Love, Sylvie

— Magic Bus, Rory MacLean

Hey Sylvie. I am going too.

PART II

EMPIRES

It is dark when I finally leave the hostel at the top of Beyoğlu and roll across the Bosphorus bridge on a night bus bound for a detour into the weird landscapes of Cappadocia.

Fitful sleep: the bus's heater goes to eleven and I am unsure if the town of Göreme is the final stop or even how many hours we have left to go. Wake up at each stop. Cold, cold air rolls in over the floor when the doors open. Somewhere along the way, I squint as the sun rises over a mirror lake.

Closer to Cappadocia, the landscape buckles and ripples. Soft hills rear up. There are weird inflections in their contours, steeper and narrower. Mountains rise from Mars-red ground. This is volcano country, and Mount Erciyes watches over it.

Around a bend in the half-pipe valleys after Nevşehir, the landscape fractures into peaks, towers, caves, castles and the "fairy chimneys".

10

FAIRYLAND

GÖREME, TURKEY

A deep layer of compressed volcanic ash covers the bedrock in Cappadocia. Millions of years ago, the ash layer was a hundred metres thick, dense but soft. As the ash was washed away through the millennia, strange rock towers remained, the same red-pink shifts as the hills. These weird towers formed under hard rocks that protected patches of dense ash from being washed away by rain and erosion, like a stone umbrella. The surrounding soft ground has been worn away, leaving the rocks on top of twisted pillars. They are called "fairy chimneys," and thousands of them dot the area around Göreme, hollowed out and perforated with small entrances and windows, used as hideaways by early Christians oppressed by the Roman empire. The ash is hard enough to support systems of caves and villages; soft enough that those caves could be carved out using nothing but wooden tools.

In the 1960's, the Hippie proto-tourists that passed through here moved into the fairy chimneys. I, too, move into a "nomad cave" hotel in Göreme. Nearby, a cave village and its many cave churches has been made into an open-air museum. In *Magic Bus*, the author revisited Cappadocia in the early '00s and climbed into a fairy chimney to stay the night – but surely that is not possible today? There must be care-takers for these caves and towers? But in Göreme, the cordoned-off museum and a few hostel/restaurant caves are the exceptions. Just ten minutes from the tourist info centre, innumerable little holes pierce the wild landscape.

Narrow, low cave churches have been carved into the weird, ice cream-like cliffs. Little cupolas and domes, vaults and pillars, and beautiful paintings of biblical scenes from early Christian myth. In the Dark Church cave, the sun has not faded the brilliant paintings at all. Like most other paintings from this region and from that time, they were vandalised during a period of religious iconoclasm. Faces have been scratched out, chunks of the soft stone broken from the walls. In some places, only the eyes have been hacked out (a disturbing effect in the dim caves), but for a different reason: the painted eyes were harvested as talismans to protect against the "evil eye". In other places names have been carved into paintings of saints for good luck, and the scraped-out plaster been used for potions that contain the essence of that saint's power.

Just kilometres from Göreme, the Selime Monastery is carved into a cliff wall. Before it carried hippies eastward to Nepal, the Silk Road carried its trade through here. Caravans moved between conveniently spaced caravanserais – ancient road motels – and stayed to freshen up and relax. Selime Monastery makes the impression of a 13th-century Best Western ("western" if you are coming from Persia, that is): six stories carved into the cliff side with dormitories, kitchens, school, defence systems, church, a camel garage and valet parking for the beasts.

I GET NO MORE than a kilometre or so along an official hike before I run into Hasan and his father, who have carved out a little wine cellar overlooking the landscape by their vineyard. A shed, a couch, a barbecue and long evenings with the sun setting in just the right place between the hills. Instead of completing my hike, I let Hasan take me to a gigantic rock castle, a hollowed-out fairy peak looming almost a hundred meters above the village of Ortahişar. We climb a nail-biting metal ladder bolted into the side of the tower, and then we disappear into ant-like tunnels and stairs inside the peak. From the top, Ortahişar is a smattering of tiny red roofs over tiny white houses, oriented along what the hills and the streets can agree on on this broken-up, bone-white ground. A deep rift runs through Ortahişar's centre, but houses and homes creep right up to its edge anyway. Hasan shows me where he lives: down there, over there, you see, and his wife works in the little hotel just down by the bend there.

Then, what the hell: Hasan's father's home-made wine straight from the plastic jerrycan he keeps in the trunk of his car.

Hasan drops me off at Sunset point again just in time to see the cracked horizon turn black in the red light, and the valley wall behind us shift from marrow-pink to dark red. I climb up a high plateau to see shadows stretch across this Martian landscape, and then I walk back under the starry, ice-cold sky, to the bed in the cave. This night I shiver under a heavy duvet with my coat as an extra cover and try to remember where I am and how I arrived here.

BEFORE SUNRISE the next cold morning, I glide in a hot air balloon through silence, broken only by the occasional whoosh of propane boosters further down the valley. We are here to see the sun rise over this bizarre landscape and there are almost fifty other balloons blooming up in the field below.

Says our pilot: "When we land later today, you will be given your own pilot certificate, so you can fly your own balloon. Just like I did yesterday!" There's frost everywhere, and we warm our cold hands on the flames that heat up the air above us. Our balloon glides down into the Love Valley.

Says our pilot: "Down there is a cemetery with Mike's customers from yesterday!"

From up here, Cappadocia is even weirder. The towers shift into plateaus shift into soft ripples shift into sharp crags. The wind is good and the balloon hops in and out of valleys one after the other; Love Valley, Rose Valley, Swords Valley... February trees below us are just black frames, but that does not stop our pilot from demonstrating how they pick apricots from the air in the summer. He attempts a low drive-by and the basket crashes through the trunk of the poor tree.

Says our pilot: "When we come closer to the ground, I want you to assume the landing position!" He demonstrates the sign of the cross.

ON THE WAY back to the cave hotel, a sign on a small restaurant advertises award-winning lentil soup. Hands frozen, feet tired. You've got a deal, mister. At the next table, an American is drinking tea and discussing travel plans with the staff. She might go to Iran one day, maybe next time. Iran, eh? Either Tehran became a charter resort while I was on the Bosphorus Express, or I am not a brave little snowflake after all.

I must leave tomorrow to catch the Trans-Asya Express from Ankara. I refuse to miss the once-a-week train again. The cook looks up from his award-winning lentils. "The to Tehran from here, you should take that. One hour north by shuttle taxi. Kayseri."

Kayseri. I *think* Kayseri is a stop on my train ticket. There's Ankara, then something, then Kayseri, then something else. Shorting out a six-hour overnight bus and six hours on the train is tempting, but if this is a mistake, I will miss the once-a-week-train again and sit stranded in the middle of Turkey.

But OK, I'll bite.

11

TRANS-ASYA EXPRESS

GÖREME, TURKEY TO TEHRAN, IRAN

A couple of hours ago, the shuttle bus driver stopped the van at a red light, opened the side door and shooed me out, dragged my backpack into the street and vanished with the green light.

Then what? Kayseri was daunting. Where is the train station? When does the train actually leave? (Does it actually leave from here?) Where can I get hold of cash, change currency, buy groceries for the 48-hour train, find wifi?

Now, Kayseri is homely. I know everything: the market is over there, the castle is from so-and-so century, the mighty and snow-covered Mount Erciyes looms as it usually does in the afternoon sun. My phone and laptop are charging on the special phone charging shelf over there.

My nervous waking over the train's departure has turned into a relaxed Ah! there is an hour left according to the departure board, so I still have time to walk down the street and stock up on some chocolate bars for the trip. The kind old man who runs the store throws in an extra box of juice since I am practically a regular customer now *(study size: n=2 visits)*. I considered leaving the laptop to charge in the station house since the good people of Kayseri wouldn't steal anything *(study size: ~20 people over two hours; observer present in the room)* and little Mustafa from the tea shop next door comes to borrow my camera again – I usually let him take a few pictures with it *(study size: n=1 times)* – and isn't it terrible how much traffic there is these days? *(study duration: since this morning)*.

The train from Ankara does roll in on time, and it does say Trans-Asya Express, and the wagon number on my ticket does exist, and the bunk number does correspond to a free bed, in a compartment with two French guys going to Tehran.

The train purser pops his head in, asks if everything is OK. He notes a missing pillow for the new traveller in the compartment – "One minute! One minute! No problem!" and disappears. "He does that every five minutes," they say, and he does say that over and over during the next two days. Then he moves me to the next-door compartment, to even out the passenger count behind each door. Instead of two fellow travellers, the compartment is shared by Saeed, a silver-haired former Iranian Air Force technician who speaks a limited set of English phrases. That is lovely, because about half of his repertoire is "More tea?", which he pours from a thermos flask.

His English warms up as we roll deeper into eastern Turkey. The train will pass five stations in about 24 hours, before making a stop at the shore of Lake Van. Cappadocia's landscape is a patch of crazy ground, but this part of Turkey is a wild expanse of mountains and valleys. In the background, snow-capped peaks; in the foreground, brown hills shot through with cherry-red patches. The train powers through valleys so steep that the sky is not visible through the windows without acrobatics. A green river follows the tracks, flushing little ice floes through the sunny plains, refreezes in the shaded valleys and thaws out again on the other side. For twelve, fourteen hours, my phone says No Service and I cannot blame it. Parts of the route could be mistaken for Switzerland, if it were not for the Turkish flag frosted onto the windows. "Yes, yes, beautiful," says Saeed, "but Iran is more beautiful. More tea?"

The train's purser pops his head in the door again. Everything OK? No problem? He has found friends for us: further back in the train is a Dutch couple, with the same outline as all of us: overland through Iran, diffuse plans to get to India. There are more like us: an Argentinian lawyer and a trio of Germans join the excited group of backpackers who throw backpacks onto the platform at the western shore of Lake Van. We embark on Orhan Atliman, a little night ferry that crosses to the other shore of Lake Van, where an Iranian train will meet us to bring us out of Turkey and close the distance to Tehran in another 24 hours or so. The sun sets just as we leave the shore, and the steep southern shore of Van turns dark blue.

The luggage wagon is the only part of the train that crosses the lake and follows us to Iran. None of us stored our belongings there, so one corner of the ferry's seating lounge is all towering backpacks, European languages, guidebooks and Saeed, who quickly adopts us, offering invaluable tips for our arrival, a crash course on Iranian post-revolutionary history and "More tea?" The little cafeteria aboard offers chocolate and cheap candy (candy is more delicious in Iran), toast (food is more delicious in Iran) and an opportunity to exchange our last Turkish currency for a stack of Iranian rial bills with a lot of zeroes on them (the exchange rate is, allegedly, more better in Iran).

Up on deck, night has turned the vast lake all black. How many times have I looked at Lake Van on maps during the past year, imagining this crossing? This night, this ferry with a train wagon aboard, far from the usual landmarks of Turkish tourism, with an Iran Raja train waiting on the other shore? Outside the little pool of light cast from the windows, the wintry night is absolutely clear and constellations in the sky are tilted all wrong in that lovely way that proves that we are far from home.

Far side of the lake: mild chaos. We all disembark and shuffle into a freezing little house. Passports and visas are given a cursory check, and the wagon/bunk numbers on the Turkey-issued tickets are scribbled out and replaced with little numbered stickers. A hundred passengers are reassigned to make sure that compartments contain only men, women, married couples or "married" couples.

Saeed promised "more delicious food" on the Iranian train that will carry us out of Turkey. Iran Raja's midnight dinner is one half of a fantastic grilled chicken, rice, bread, something to drink, tea and cookies. A number of rials (many zeroes), something like one Euro, buys the dinner.

Around 3AM we check out from Turkey. Yet another coats-on, snowy-platform, fluorescent light-fitted station house with border police who do not bother to show up until much later. We are not allowed across the border just yet. Iranian customs are checking the bags. Oh boy, the stories about Iranian customs checks. Not only do they allegedly comb the luggage wagon for anything funny brought home from the party metropolis of Istanbul, they check all sorts of things on amoral Westerners. I was advised to create a separate, clean Facebook account, delete apps from the phone, create a user account on the laptop without music or suspicious e-books. Recall the Bulgarian border guard: "if you hesitate like that in Iran..."

I rehearse the address to the hotel, but the booking hasn't been confirmed yet... what if they call ahead? Should I have left my alcohol-based cologne in Turkey? Ridiculous, yes, but being sleep-deprived on a freezing border station in the night with a train swirling in film noir smoke receding into mist, while border guard silhouettes go through the luggage in the train...

An hour later, almost at five in the morning, we play the passport/visa check game at the Iranian border at Razi. The Bulgarian border check was "authentic." The Turks were suspicious about my passport's Turkish exit stamp. The Iranians are going to have a party with my visa, because the portrait on it clearly depicts a career criminal. I rehearse the hotel address, Amir Kabir street, exit dates, ten days from now, but damnit, I do not have an onward ticket, and the hotel booking is not confirmed and, and, and…

They collect the passport on the train. No-one seems to have bothered with the 65 litres of potential contraband on my bunk bed with my name on it. We go to sleep. They knock on the door about an hour later and hand it back with a polite "Welcome in Iran, mister." I am *disappointed*.

The train crawls along the foothills of the Alborz mountains, to Tehran. A thirty-minute halt for prayers in Tabriz. Stretching out like cats in fresh, sharp sunlight, the tourists bunch out as well. A chance to walk up and down the platform to raise the pulse and flush out stagnant blood in arteries to tense muscles. It has been 48 hours and it is starting to show on us ragged passengers on the Trans-Asya Express. Some file off to the station mosque – just a few, travellers are exempt from prayers – and even more run off to the hopefully cleaner bathrooms. The train's bathrooms are currently not places where you would enjoy brushing your teeth. It is at least another twelve hours until we reach the capital, and we should expect some delays. Maybe arrive around ten, maybe just after midnight. The subway closes at 11.

We stop for prayers and fresh air a few more times, but after just one or two stops, it is dark outside again and another day has passed in the compartments. We go to the restaurant a bit further back in the train and clear out what little food they have left. Then we just crunch out the last hours. We compare station names with Lonely Planet to see roughly where we are, but it is hard to project an arrival time. The train moves quickly in places, slowly in places, and there is a long southward curve at the end where the train approaches from the west, circles around Tehran to arrive from the south. Slightly bent over in the couchettes or straightening up in the corridor while pretending to see anything in the black outside. Open windows to clear out the air – there is a blue mist in the corridor as the No Smoking sign has turned from a rule to a reminder to a recommendation to a suggestion to a mockery.

Just before midnight, the lights that glide by on the sides of the tracks turn urban. Sometime around half past, we finally arrive at Tehran's central train station where the air is heavy with petroleum. The station house is desert-hot, heated by gas-fired radiators at full blast. A flurry of goodbyes and well-wishes to and from our Iranian friends from the train, who will wait for their baggage in the still-Turkish luggage wagon to be delivered on airport-style conveyor belts. We lose track of the French, but the Dutch couple, the lawyer from Argentina and I are led to a taxi by someone that someone knows. We are taken to our hotel through empty streets inside a very small thing on wheels. Clown car-style, with our helper crawling into what he calls "the middle front seat" – that is, on top of the handbrake. All our possessions are strapped to the roof with bungee cord. I am happy my bag is a bit too heavy.

12

TRYING TEHRAN

TEHRAN, IRAN

Walking just a few minutes down Ferdozeh street towards Imam Khomeini square, the strangest thing in Tehran becomes obvious: that it is a normal city (with a traffic problem).

Sure, every free surface has one or two white beards looking down at us, one friendly, one stern. Ayatollahs Khomeini and Khamenei are everywhere. The rest is air pollution, LED signboards, hawkers selling everything and anything, and heavy traffic.

The first time a motorbike comes down the sidewalk is a surprise. The first U-turn into oncoming traffic is a surprise. The first realisation that street lane directions are not really agreed on, a surprise. The first street-crossing is toe-curling. The first time I cross a street at night, I hear myself whimper as headlights zip by, far too close.

A word search for "traffic" in my guidebook to Iran returns the following wordings: "Given the diabolical nature of traffic in Iran," "the maelstrom of traffic," "five lanes of cacophonous traffic," "a city literally choking to death on chronic pollution and endless traffic jams" and "a Darwinian game of chicken." In this city where traffic directions are a suggestion, even the green traffic light is labelled "Cross with care".

In the river of millions of little Honda motorbikes, try to find older Tehranis and cross the street with them. It will not be any less scary, but it is comforting to see that even pedestrians live to see their forties in Tehran. The desperate cynic can cross downstream from someone carrying a small child. After making an infant your human shield, the crushing guilt is a very good motivation for your next crossing! If all else fails, remember the guidebook's merry affirmation that a driver "will do anything to avoid running you over simply because doing so is just too much of a hassle."

Tehran's zebra crossings are a lot safer to spectate from inside – inside one of four vehicles making staggered U-turns into oncoming traffic, cutting off and blocking a city bus while a motorbike comes down the lane the wrong way. Drivers try to break this life-sized Sokoban puzzle by honking. A man weaves his way through traffic, selling newspapers to those who are stuck in gridlock.

Everything is new and everything old was wrong and it is humbling. Unexpected for a city of this size: strangers on the subway slice 20 minutes off their day to make sure we find our way to the Azadi tower. Expected for a city this size: people eating fast food while walking, or advertisements for home insurance. War propaganda reels repeat on the TV while we have breakfast. Snack-sized sheep brains with green pepper are served as fast food alongside falafel and hamburgers.

I let my guard down and soon I sit cross legged on a couch among new friends, getting a crash course in the dynamics of running a small business in Tehran, sipping tea and browsing through a volume of Khayyam, fed samples of Iranian candy in the makeshift office of a budding wholesale candy shop. They refuse to let me leave without a full bag of samples, too. All of this under the ægis of the boyfriend of a friend of an Iranian woman from the hostel in Istanbul a week earlier. A third-order acquaintance worked a night shift to be able to guide me for a full day.

"Careful with the camera," I read before coming here, "they might think you are a journalist". Police will stop you in the street and arrest you as a spy and you will spend your thirties interrogated in a secret bunker in Natanz. Sure, stopped in the street, definitely – in the middle of the night by an old man who wants to say hello in English and share his little bag of walnuts. And, surprise, stopped in the street by Emeric and Florian, the French guys from the train, because apparently this city of 15-20 million inhabitants is small enough to run into them on a midnight walk down a backstreet.

Another commuter leads us up from the subway and helps us find the Grand Bazaar in Tehran. We emerge from the underground into a crowd, a throng, a rally! Where are all these people going? Something must have happened! We are in the middle of a protest! My government *specifically* warns against going into masses of people like this! But this is the regular market crowd. Outside the bazaar. On a Monday afternoon. The grand bazaar is ancient – age unknown. The bazaris are typically religious and conservative, with an air of old, old Persia. But as with everything else, the bazaar is filled with both old men running century-old spice shops, and filled with old men streaming football on smartphones. When we turn a corner in the Grand Bazaar and end up in the lingerie block to find half a dozen giggling women covered by full *chador* browsing for Stars and Stripes-printed underwear, I surrender.

I surrender to Valiasr Street with its 17 kilometres of densely planted trees and little canals on each side. The Alborz range as a backdrop. Surrender to the calm of Tajrish bazaar. The Love Bridge. The study hall at the university in a winter garden under a greenhouse roof where tiny birds sing indoors. Walking and talking through streets lit by LED signs where Tehranis eat ice-cream in early February.

> For those who have grown up on an endless diet of images depicting Iran as a dark, dangerous place full of fundamentalist fanatics, discovering the real Iran is the most wonderful surprise.
> ... a journey in Iran will change the way you see this part of the world.
>
> — Lonely Planet: Iran

"Is it OK to take a photo of the mountains?" is the dumbest question I have ever asked but everything I knew is wrong.

"Why are there so few mosques in Tehran and so many in Turkey?" I ask. "We're not like them, not as religious."

I am silent for ten minutes while my brain pages out old, useless knowledge from my cortex. Over lunch a news clip from government media rolls patriotic messages for tomorrow's celebrations of the Revolution. As I mash the second act of the *abgoosht*, a lamb stew eaten in stages, on my plate, Obama flickers by on TV. Scary soundtrack, horror-movie colour grading and cherrypicked soundbites from his speech. This reverse culture shock is exhausting.

Late evening, I am led to the Little Bazaar under the starry sky and trees in Laleh park. It is illuminated like an amusement park and there's soft music somewhere behind the trees and a million Chinese trinkets are on sale and it is almost summer tonight. We walk through the park where silhouettes play backgammon and ping-pong. There is a playground, with a jungle gym covered in kids out past bedtime. By the skating rink there is a little girl in all pink stumbling around in circles under floodlights. It is embarrassing to explain that I did not expect to see kids with rollerblades and my new friends smile and laugh and say they are happy I like the park.

They drop me off at Ferdozeh square. It is tricky to get to my hotel because we can't make a right turn here and... is it OK? Can you walk from here? They wave good-bye from a dark car under all the neon lights. It is a ten-minute walk among Tehranis, street food stands and green-white-red illuminations.

The hotel lobby is empty, musty. The smell of gas-fired radiators linger. A long day deserves a long night.

"Mister, this is for you!"

I forgot the bag of candy samples in the car, but somehow it has already been delivered to the hotel reception.

13

DEN OF ESPIONAGE

TEHRAN, IRAN

"Mister S. will come soon," chirps the guard who just denied us entry into the museum. When Mister S. comes, we will see if we can be allowed in. The former US embassy, where the staff was taken hostage in 1979 and held for over a year, has been turned into a museum, charmingly named the "US Den of Espionage." This brick building behind a very spiky fence is sacred ground for conservative Iranians and Americans alike.

A problem: the museum is only open during one weekend per year. Luckily, it is this weekend. Another problem: we missed the opening hours yesterday and today it is closed.

Damien, the Argentinian lawyer from the train, is comfortable around authority and paperwork. He unfolds a crumpled note with a name and number – Mister S.' name and number – and implies that we have a personal invitation from the museum director. We do not, of course. On the scrap of paper is no more than "no, but call this number tomorrow and ask again".

Mister S. does not show up, and our guard apologises for his supervisor being late. He opens the gate for cars passing in and out of the compound, mostly men who smile and wave as they pass. He does not know much about the museum. It is no big deal, just things and rooms, okay? But we would really like to see the things and rooms, if possible.

Eventually, Mister S. shows up. There is a bit of Farsi discussion between the two; the "come on, they've waited a long time" argument falls in our favour. Mister S. asks for our nationalities, and with a friendly handshake and welcome he leads us up the stairs over a door mat that reads "DOWN WITH USA".

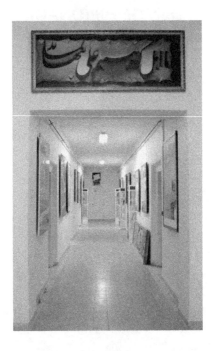

Mister S. does not speak much English, so he drops us off in CIA's former office and goes off to look for someone who does. To skulk around the dark rooms with glass cabinets full of old radio equipment, document destroyers, books and a collection of propaganda art, is like playing hide and seek in a most bizarre arena.

Ten minutes later, a younger version of Mister S. appears and guides us through the entire place, showing and demonstrating whichever machinery has moving parts: code room doors, camera filters, printing presses. The infamous Glass Room with its transparent, un-buggable walls, trapping argon gas between plates of plexi to make sound transport and eavesdropping impossible.

Shredded documents that have been reconstructed by carpet weavers. The separated crypto cages, metal rooms with surprisingly advanced authentication mechanisms: code, weight plate sensor and iris scanners – all from the mid-seventies. Here is the staircase where embassy staff escaped during the hostage crisis. Here is a paper shredder filled to the brim with flakes of paper. Here is a workbench presented as a forgery workshop. Here is a glass case filled with crypto equipment. Here is a Statue of Liberty with a grinning skull face and a model prison in her cell torso. A bizarre museum indeed.

Back outside, Damien stands in the middle of traffic and photographs something that should not be photographed, until a policeman politely asks him not to.

14
ASIDE: PRODUCT PLACEMENT

A microfibre towel, size Small.

Usage: 40 by 60 cm, enough to dry off one newly showered backpacker and dries completely hanging off the backpack for ten minutes.
Results: Preliminary results show that the towel can mop up a lake of water that poured out the back of a refrigerator in a hotel room because I pulled the plug on it in the middle of the night in a desperate attempt to get it to STOP MAKING THAT NOISE.
   Circumstances: Indications suggest that it performs well even if check-out time from the hotel is "pretty damn soon".
   Future work: This trial will hopefully never be repeated.

15

THE EARLY BIRD IS TOO EARLY

TEHRAN TO ISFAHAN, IRAN

> We are already some farsakhs from Teherán when day breaks on the 4th of February, 1889. The start is not a propitious one. Hardly have we cleared the Ispahán gate than down comes the Shagird's horse as if he were shot, breaking his girths and rider's thumb at the same moment. Luckily, we are provided with rope, and Persian saddles are not complicated.
>
> — A RIDE TO INDIA ACROSS PERSIA AND BALUCHISTÁN, HARRY DE WINDT (1891)

This start is more "propitious". Check out from the hotel, take the Metro to Terminal-e Jonoub, listen for a bus caller to yell "Isfahaaan!", throw the backpack into the bus's underbelly and pay the ticket. We follow a wide south-bound highway out of Tehran, whose suburbs end abruptly in dark flatland. Sometime during the night, we pass by the infamous uranium enrichment facility in Natanz.

Overnight buses are just as convenient as night trains: depart late at night, sleep, and arrive around breakfast. I have slept in worse hotel rooms than this "VIP" bus, which serves complimentary dinner and newspapers, but there is an unexpected downside. They are a lot faster than the normal buses, so we arrive long before breakfast. When the bus pulls into the terminal and someone politely wakes me up, it is still dark out. It is four in the pitch-dark morning in Kaveh Central, five kilometres outside Isfahan. The city lies in I have no idea which direction, and I am not well rested yet. This start just became less propitious.

I need to sleep before I figure out the next steps. Kaveh Central bus terminal has a motel, with available beds. The night clerk insists that even if I check in at four in the morning, the check-out time still is at noon. Fairly sure that checking into a bus stop motel in the middle of the night and paying by the hour does not looks good.

At dawn, I walk the last kilometres into Isfahan as it awakens to the last day of the celebration of the revolution. Everyone is coming out for parade and picnic, including the motorcycle club "Ninja Rangers".

I pause to look at the anti-USA propaganda on this big day. Some pre-printed "DOWN WITH USA" and "We don't trust the United States" signs are handed out along with merry paper hats in green-white-red.

I stand in the same place on the sidewalk in Isfahan for a long while, just looking at it all, until a cheerful gentleman appears from a door behind me, pulls me into his hostel and sells me on a dorm bed. In the hostel's inner garden: the French guys again. Am I their stalker?

16

ASIDE: ECONOMY OF SCALE

Shopping streets and districts in this part of the world confuse me. Stores that sell the same thing are bunched up in the same place. There will be five electronic shops in a row, a district for shoes, two guys selling plumbing material off a tarp in the street, right next to each other. Why would you open another audio mixer table store right where the need is obviously saturated?

Of course, at this population scale, there is no difference between seven or eight kitchen faucets shops in a row. Better to establish a geographic location for pencil sharpeners, or a high-street niche store selling only a narrow selection of nuts.

That said, I will always wonder what market forces caused Isfahan's exclusive saucepans-and-plush-toys street happen.

17

SAY YES, YES MAN

ISFAHAN, IRAN

We all want to be the sort of *wonderful*, positive and affirmative person who just says Yes! to whatever crazy and wild *adventures* life throws your way – especially when doing something as *delightful* as discovering new *exotic* places by yourself with only a backpack and a vague plan.

It is to grow, to find secret places in the world, to wake up in a new city, to meet new souls and try exotic food and to walk barefoot in the sands of mother Gaia's beaches and to feel freedom between the toes and to lose sight of the shore. To not be bound by norms, to break free from, y'know, grinding 9-to-5 *society*.

Follow your own heart, your dreams, your childish sense of wonder. Don't look back, because there's nothing there! Go where life takes you! Run with the wolves and listen to the little voice that says to dare, that whispers *go for it*. To get lost, to see the sunrise over inspirational messages that tell you to *Do Everything, Regret Nothing* in that jagged font that flower shops use.

Yeah, the "say yes" strategy tends to end up in a gift shop that has a special tourist pricing for a limited time only. But it also ends up warm dialogue with a five-year old kid practicing his English on ragged backpackers, repeatedly quizzing where we are from, our names and Where are you from again mister, I forgot; all the while his father proudly records the conversation on his phone.

Saying yes leads to a combination of both: an honest step closer to the everyday life, *and* an opportunity for you to purchase a very reasonably priced carpet that is only set at this price today for whatever reason. Please, have some tea! Yes, the spontaneous afternoon with an enthusiastic driver and guide in Cappadocia (and the home-brewed wine straight from the plastic jerrycan in the trunk of his car) did end with a visit to a local carpet factory and some very special offers for me only.

That is fine. Saying yes to someone who claims to be a bazaar elder (hah!) who wants to show us around the bazaar (how convenient!) will end up in some special places (like your nephew's boutique, I guess?) because we are good friends now (all of ten minutes). But what the hell, let's go. And sure enough, we end up in some uncle's workshop producing hand-stamped traditional Persian tablecloths. But before that we are led up a set of winding stone stairs, through tilting floors of busy back-offices and noisy workshops, up to the sun-warmed, quiet roof of the 17th-century bazaar that surrounds the Naqsh-e Jahan square in Isfahan.

The Sheikh Lotfollah mosque sits off to one side of the Naqsh-e Jahan square in Isfahan. It is a small, humble dome without minarets, curiously angled away from the eastern wall of the square.

Inside: that delightful but strict math of great architecture. The prayer hall of the Lotfollah mosque is a square: four walls. From the four corners in-between those four walls rise eight arches and eight curved triangles, which split into sixteen points along the rim of the dome. Sixteen windows spill different light into the hall over the course of the day, which is reflected in thirty-two instances of a tiled pattern that repeats all the way up to the apex of the dome, where glazed and unglazed tiles shrink the pattern until it fractures into a colourful mosaic foam at the top.

One hall, two cardinal axes, four corners, eight arches, sixteen windows, thirty-two pattern copies in sixty-four glazed and unglazed parts. Tidy powers of two: $2^0, 2^1, 2^2, 2^3, 2^4, 2^5, 2^6$.

Robert Byron celebrated Lotfollah mosque's tiling and decoration, placing it alongside Versailles, St Peter's cathedral and the Doge's palace in Venice.

> On the right rises that brick boot-box the Ali Gapu; opposite, the flowered saucer dome of the Mosque of Sheikh Lutfullah, skewed sideways over a blue recess. Symmetry, but not too much. ... But the beauty of the whole comes as you move. The highlights are broken by the play of glazed and unglazed surfaces, so that with every step they rearrange themselves in countless shining patters.
>
> — ROAD TO OXIANA, ROBERT BYRON (1937)

There are many things to see in Isfahan: the striking domes of the mosques around the Naqsh-e Jahan square, the play of fountains, the sunlight-and-dark contrasts of the bazaars' corridors, the winding tunnels in the backstreets behind it, the colourful flags and lights of celebrations, the walk along the Zayandeh river and the secret bookshop hidden in a vault under a bridge, the street side falafel, the trinket-filled teahouse in a basement, the gentle crowds, the cool evenings and the sweet, sweet tea to go with them. The Chehel Sotoun ("Forty columns") palace with twenty columns at its entrance and the remaining twenty reflected in the surface of a pool.

But my favourite sight guards the Museum of Natural History. Of all the things in Isfahan, I love this dinosaur the most.

18

ASIDE: UNLICENSED TAXIS

Extending my visa in Isfahan requires a trip to the police station to request the extension. The hostel drives me across the city through the early morning streets, the city waking up as we pass through empty streets.

My extension is denied because there is too much time left on the visa; extensions are only granted in the last three days of the allowed stay. After a visit to the police, I am back on the street at the other end of the city. I have the address to the Amir Kabir hostel on a Post-It note in my passport.

Licensed taxis are either green or yellow. Posters warn tourists against taking unlicensed taxis in other colours – it can become "very expensive". A taxi driver leans on the hood of one of the green taxis just outside the police station. After I ask for a ride back, he jogs across the street, hops into his black unlicensed taxi parked on the other side, and burns rubber through a tight U-turn. He opens the passenger door and shoos me in. At least I *tried* to do the right thing.

I have tried to be suspicious and careful, but I am unable to. In the still-early morning he speeds down the highway back towards northern Isfahan, blasting Metallica through tinny speakers.

19

HOPEFULLY UNDER CONSTRUCTION
ISFAHAN TO SHIRAZ, IRAN

I yawn in synch with the French as our night bus pulls into a station in early, early morning hours. We have arrived in Shiraz with only a vague sense of direction and an unclear position on a map in a PDF file on a phone that is low on battery. A French vagabond couple that we met on the ferry across Lake Van in Turkey has joined us. Small sub-continent, this. An unlikely reunion. They are hitchhiking and camping their way to Australia. Between the guys making their way to China overland and this couple tearing across the globe in a tent, this might as well be a charter buddy trip to Las Palmas.

Oh wait! Here comes Damien too, our Argentinian friend from Tehran. He was nowhere to be found when we ran for the bus last night, but here he is..! We are six people now, all from the same train and travelling at the same pace. We walk towards Shiraz as the sun comes up, looking for somewhere to sleep.

"No hotel", says a hotel owner.

Granted, it *looks* like he is right: the lobby might have been a bomb shelter once... but the door is marked HOTEL and he did open the door to six tired backpackers. Come *on*. He relents and quotes us a price on a scrap of paper: extremely cheap, even for Iran. The note must be missing a zero at the end. After vigorous sign language he insists that the price is correct, and that it is the total price for all six of us.

We follow him up a spiral staircase where the steps just stick out of the wall of the stairwell. This place must be under total remodelling, because no, the staircase has no railing.

We plop into a couch in the owner's office at six in the morning. While most of us nod off into micro-sleep, there is a full five minutes of confused hand-waving over whether they really have any free rooms in the building. Do they think we just came to look around? We certainly do not look like hotel inspectors. Someone is snoring on the couch already. I breathe deeply to stay awake for another minute. *Come on.* Are there rooms for six people? The phrase book helps us with our request: *how much is a... do you one...*

three room... have hotel? Farsi is hard. Er, rooms for five people. Damien has disappeared, again.

Insects, questionable electricity, spotty hospital corridor lighting. The beds are MDF board lined with plywood. The corridors may be the original decor from a horror movie. We prepare a simple breakfast of biscuits and tea over the vagabond couple's camping stove. It burns with a merry flame – in their room, on the carpet. This hotel would be improved by fire, if only to clear out the insects. Wrapped in my travel bedsheets and covered in imagined(?) itchy-scratchy from bedbugs, I wonder if it had been worth the effort to invest another 30 minutes to find this hotel instead:

> The city's only traditional hotel is located in the heart of the old quarter and is a fantastical choice. You can sleep in the clean and comfortable dorm or in a private room – some are arranged around the central courtyard of the original house...
>
> — Lonely Planet: Iran

...and something about an excellent restaurant something coffeeshop wifi and air conditioning. In the morning, the shower head in our room falls clean out of the bathroom wall.

20

THE PRAGMATIC SHRINE

SHIRAZ, IRAN

We take a walk to see if we can find Damien a fifth time. A labyrinth of narrow backstreets and tunnels leads into a traditional building complex and to the courtyard of that top-rated guesthouse – it is a guess as good as any. Sure, an Argentinian was here just a moment ago! But oh, he already left, and with that he is gone.

Close by is the Madrasah-e Khan, a theological university that has been active since its construction in 1615. A group of imams mill about outside a mosque after the Friday prayer, and one of them offers to take us there. The guidebook offers the following:

> **Opening hours:** knock on the door. The doors are usually closed but if you are lucky the caretaker will open it.

We knock, and wait. A toothless elder opens the door after a while, asks a hefty fee for the favour and lets us into the inner courtyard: all stillness, shade and blooming orange trees. We are left alone to wander lecture halls, corridors, little study cells and fourth-floor walkways (of course, no railing). A narrow staircase and a bundle of electrical wiring hanging loose are the marks of a school under renovation.

Behind another bundle of wiring and light fixtures, behind

another door ajar, behind another narrow staircase, blinding sunlight pours from the top end of a ladder. We climb up and out on top of the madrassa's walls and look down into its garden. Continue around its perimeter, explore a spiral staircase ending in a dark cell, admire glazed mosaic walls, count the surrounding construction cranes. A high step, a little push and a jump takes us yet a bit further up on the arched summit of the building.

We stay for a long while in the high air. Sitting here on a stolen afternoon on a roof behind a discreet door in a madrasah in Iran, it finally feels possible that the vagabond couple will somehow make it on their hitchhike to Australia, that the French guys will make it along the entire ancient Silk Road to China, and that I will somehow make it to Kathmandu in a month or two.

IN THE CENTRE of Shiraz sits Shah Cheragh, one of the holiest sites of Shia Islam. Reportedly, non-Muslims are not allowed to enter, but we make an attempt anyway. No cameras allowed, strict dress code, separate entrance for women, the whole nine. We approach attentively, read the place, the crowd, the authorities, the atmosphere. No problem. A guard wielding a rainbow-coloured dusting brush ushers us heathens toward a counter where we can hand in our cameras. This is just before the Friday prayers in Iran's top-holy shrine. This is going to be juicy.

But again, even this ultra-holy mosque complex is down-to-

Earth. Under the massive domes and towering minarets, kids drive toy cars on the warm red carpets and shimmering tile-work. There is a small common kitchen behind a small library. Divine works of architecture and spiritual rigour, but also welcoming social spaces of sure, step right in, please take your shoes off.

Here, two sons of the seventh imam lie in a mausoleum that no-one turns their backs to: crowds crab-walk past it. Walls and ceilings covered in millions of tiny mirror shards shimmer, glint, reflect and refract everything. The faithful man on his knees is re-imaged in mirror mosaic all over this hall. The walls sparkle red, green, prismatic violet and cold blue winter skies bounce all the way in here from the outside when the doors open.

But: in this fantastic mirror palace, a simple wooden shelf and electric outlets has been bolted straight into the mirror glass so the praying can charge their phones. While adults recite the beginning of the Quran with their foreheads pressed against this very special carpet, their children play on it. A mobile scissor lift platform drives around indoors during the Friday prayer, so a caretaker can polish the splendent ceiling.

Salaat – prayers – are said in thirty-four reps by people who come here five times a day, though Shia Islam permits performing the noon and afternoon prayers back-to-back to avoid an extra trip to a prayer room if it is inconvenient. The time slots, *waqt*, were traditionally tracked against the position of the sun, but there is a GPS app for that now. The dress code ranges from formal to sweatpants. The awkward buzzing of someone who forgot to silence their cellphone before entering. Coming here is like going to a gym for the spirit: a simple thing, part of routine.

Back in the courtyard outside, families are gathered to picnic on carpets, sharing their pistachio nuts with us. We are picked up by a guide who enthusiastically explains the architecture and history of the place. Ah, it is such a pity that cameras are forbidden in here, it would have been lovely to have a picture of the mirror mosque to show back home. "Oh", says the guide. She collects our email addresses in a notebook and sends us a set of jpgs.

21

MR. O

SHIRAZ, IRAN

We meet Mr. O and his wife on the carpets outside the Shah Cheragh. In three minutes, he invites us dirty backpackers to dinner at his home here in Shiraz.

The seven of us navigate the bazaar as Mr. O talks without pause and suggests going to the cinema before dinner to see an Iranian film in a proper theatre but his wife counters that we can see a movie whenever we like and then we come out in the street and Mr. O suggests that we grab a snack like a sandwich or a pizza before we go home but it's OK, let's just go straight to dinner and so we debate taking a taxi or going by bus – the bus seems better, since all of us would require two taxis – and after a few bus stops he waves at us to get out and we pile into the street where Mr. O apologizes for his English and gets the bright idea to buy an English-Farsi lexicon at the little bookshop tent right here and we wait for a moment while he intensely browses the selection until he informs us that he needs to split a large bill to be able to pay for the book and he storms off down the street and it's almost ten minutes until he comes barging back around the corner, but there's some problem with the payment and so he disappears running full tilt in the other direction and is gone again while his patient wife looks like this has happened before and when he comes back his phone is dead but there's another battery and a brief exchange of phone numbers before we head off to the next bus stop where, after three or four buses pass, we start to feel like he does not really know the way to their home because everything seems so confused between him and his patient, patient wife, but the wait is put to good use: we rehearse the English names for all the animals in the two paint-by-numbers booklets for children he bought at the bookshop and then Mr. O suggests that we all crash at his place tonight after dinner? before his question "maybe we should get a taxi?" further strengthens the suspicion that Mr. O does not know which bus to take from here but of course we climb aboard a bus again and go something like 200 meters before he orders everyone off again to take a look at Hafez' mausoleum as a side trip but we already have a date to visit it tomorrow so instead it's time for a snack or a noodle soup on the sidewalk outside the tomb in the streetlight and, hm, he says, it's getting late and Mr. O's home is still some distance away, so, he suggests, how about we meet for dinner tomorrow instead and then all of us can sleep at his home, hm? after which he and his patient, patient wife walks us all the way back to the hotel which makes almost an hour's walk back to where we started this adventure and see you at Hafez' Tomb tomorrow around three o'clock, OK?

We probably missed some aspect of the *tarouf* code of radical courtesy whereby we were expected to decline Mr. O's invitation, because the next day, Mr. O is nowhere to be found.

22

THERE ARE DOGS AT PERSEPOLIS!

PERSEPOLIS, IRAN

All five of us, plus the driver, can fit into a regular taxi car if we sit on top of each other. We pile in and speed out on the highway. We go towards Persepolis, the colossal remains of the ancient capital of king Darius I, in the vast, dry Marvdasht plains outside Shiraz. After travelling city to city by night bus, I now see the countryside of the first time: dusty and bleak in the low morning, but warming into friendly earth tones and patches of green forest. Occasionally, we pass wide flatbed trucks carrying battle tanks down the highway.

The taxi stops suddenly by a ticket booth at the foot of the mighty Persepolis platform. A flat, wide staircase leads up onto it and through the Gate of Nations, covered in Xerxes' royal inscriptions, and graffiti scratched in by 19th-century explorers. Through the gate we come into a 2500-year old forest of pillars, crumbled arches and enormous sandstone statues.

Persepolis' massive platform served as the capital of the Achaemenid empire with its collection of palaces, diplomatic halls. It served as the (literally epic) centre of the Persian nation – until Alexander destroyed it:

> While they were feasting and the drinking was far advanced, as they began to be drunken, a madness took possession of the minds of the intoxicated guests. At this point one of the women present, Thais by name and Athenian by origin, said that for Alexander it would be the finest of all his feats in Asia if he joined them in a triumphal procession, set fire to the palaces, and permitted women's hands in a minute to extinguish the famed accomplishments of the Persians.
>
> — HISTORICAL LIBRARY, DIODORUS (C:A 60 BCE)

Persepolis is one of the finest places to visit in the Middle East. It makes manifest the memory of lost empires, of warrior kings, of high culture, all in stark, dignified scenery. Persepolis stands as it did, with only a ticket booth at the foot of the platform, some railings around the most fragile monuments, an exhibition of found objects of archaeological importance and with a few plaques spelling out explanations in Farsi only.

At the far end of the capital is a kiosk serving coffee. Business is slow. Olivier, the transcontinental vagabond, plays a few games of backgammon with its owner before we are besieged by a class of schoolboys on a field trip who want to practice their English.

Curious kids ask us where we are from, while their proud teachers apologise for disturbing us.

It is seven or eight kilometres from Persepolis to the royal necropolis at Naqsh-e Rostam, and we intend to walk there because we have all day and the weather is nice. When Florian asks a nearby taxi driver for the way to Rostam, the taxi is immediately available to drive us there, and it takes vigorous repetition and non-verbal communication to demonstrate that we intend to walk to Rostam and that yes, there is something wrong with us. Smelling hard-line bargainers, the taxi driver offers a very good deal. But we are still walking. How about this: he offers to drive us to Rostam and wait there for a couple of hours, then drive back to Shiraz, for the same price as going directly to Shiraz?

The taxi driver probably considers a psycho-clinical explanation, but the deal is sealed: we walk the seven-or-eight kilometres to Rostam, he picks us up in three hours and drives us to Shiraz. Twenty minutes down the road in the strong sunlight, we decline another offer to drive us the remainder of the dusty route. Florian uses the same non-verbal finger-walking and side-of-head-tapping to explain that we are still walking to Rostam. "But there are dogs," the driver protests. Armed with rocks, we continue down the road. The dangerous dogs turn out to be unusually furry sheep.

We rest at the ancient tombs of Darius I and II, Xerxes I and Artaxerxes I, indulge in ice-cream and yell hello to the same school bus full of the same kids again as it pulls up to visit the tombs.

The taxi driver shows up fifteen minutes ahead of schedule, thunders down the highway to Shiraz, and immediately gets a flat tire in the middle of the Marvdasht nowhere. As we stand gathered around the taxi, the school bus filled with waving kids passes us a third time.

23

THE OFFICE OF ALIEN AFFAIRS
SHIRAZ, IRAN

The directions say to walk down this way, turn into the third alley on the left, walk through the green door and head up to the third floor. I walk through the green door of a government-looking building. People stream in and out with papers and folders, and official posters decorate the walls, but nothing says "visa" or "alien affairs" as far as I can see – everything is in Farsi. I try to ask around for the foreign affairs office using that word I picked up: "Farangi? Farangi?"

The building I am scouting is not the foreign affairs office. *Ha ha. No no.* It is the social security office, a woman informs me after I barge into her office, asking for "Foreigner? Foreigner?" Staff members kindly help this visibly lost *farangi* into a taxi to the office where foreigners are processed.

But the taxi drives twenty minutes down the highway, out of Shiraz, and drops me off outside another building that is definitely not the right place at all, again. This building is the General Office of Immigration, and the machine gun-carrying guard outside patiently explains that it does *not* handle visa extensions…

Another taxi to the correct street, through the correct green door, and up to the correct third floor. This time, the third floor is full of applicants powering through visa issues in order to stay in

Iran. Migrant workers, relatives, asylum seekers, special protection errands and then me who just wants to extend my vacation, please?

In overview, the process is straightforward:

1. go to the Office of Alien Affairs and apply for an extension
2. go to Melli Bank in Shohada square and pay the processing fee
3. bring the receipt back to the police
4. get the extension stamped into the passport
5. boom, done

I queue up politely at the back of the line until someone takes pity on the naïve farangi who believes in queuing and pulls me up to the counter by the sleeve, skipping at least fifteen people. There is no queue system. The "queue" is an illusion, just people standing along a wall in various stages of approval, approaching an array of desks over and over as their names are called.

After a short interview about my reasons for extending the visa I receive a little slip of paper and get directed to "Management". Management is in a sunny corner office where I am interviewed again by a senior police officer, who stamps the paper and fills out an extension application for me. Return to the waiting room to stand in line (again), get pulled to the front (again) to hand in the application.

Next step: go to Melli Bank to pay the processing fee. The guards outside the office gesture towards a green "special taxi", engine running. A proper, licensed cab!

But we do not go towards Shohada square at all. The taxi peels around the corner and into backstreets and no no no, not back out of town again, *please*! I was so close to sorting this out! "Melli Bank?" I ask weakly. "One minute," the driver assures me, and a literal minute later he pulls up outside a Melli Bank office in a suburb. Come, come, come! I try to keep up with him as he jogs past long lines at the counters. He waves hello! to the manager of the bank, cuts to the front of a line, pushes a customer aside at the counter, physically reaches behind the counter to produce the necessary forms and fill them out for me with rapid-fire questions: name? country? father's name? "Money!" he barks, snatches my fistful of bills and counts up the money, pays the fee, finishes up, grabs the payment receipt and then we jog back out to his taxi.

He swings by a copy shop on the way back, disappears inside, leaving me in his car with the engine running, comes back with copies of all the documents I need duplicated, and drops me back outside the police office in fifteen minutes flat.

Documents, passport photos, proof of residence, bank receipt and copies, all in a pink cover folder, are handed in to an officer. Hundreds of pink folders lay piled up and scattered across the tables, pile up again and scatter again. My name is called once or twice to answer questions and sign papers. Doors slam. Chairs creak. Names are called. Stamps go click-bang-click. Papers are shuffled. My little crimson passport makes glacial progress closer to the last officer in line.

It is painfully obvious that having a Scandinavian passport is Easy Mode. No-one questions its validity, no-one asks tough questions about stamps or dates, no-one scoffs at the country on the cover, no-one challenges my reasons for staying – unlike the people around me with important and difficult errands. Asylum seekers, applying for special protection, medical reasons. Pakistani, Iraqi, Lebanese, Afghani passports.

I have no idea how long this process takes. Whoever decorated this waiting room mercifully chose not to put up a clock anywhere.

24

SUNRISE ON THE GULF

SHIRAZ TO BANDAR ABBAS, IRAN

My bus for Bandar Abbas leaves at nine in the evening. The Frenchmen roll towards Kerman at ten. The vagabond couple leave for Yazd at eleven. Five polystyrene cups of tea on a bench outside the bus terminal, and I remember the saffron-flavoured sugar rocks I got from the candy store in Tehran. A bus driver sweeps in and helps himself to a fistful of them. We plop the rest of the saffron into the most decadent teacups and enjoy them on a bench.

It is that time again; the time to shrug on backpacks and disappear in different directions, and as melancholic as ever. The shittiest part of solo travel is the constant separations. But just as I cosy up in the bus and try to figure out how to lean back the seat, a familiar French face pops back onboard and "We found company for you, she studies English in Bandar Abbas!" and there is *salaam*, how do you do. I guess you are never alone.

THE NIGHT BUS PULLS IN, as usual, to a stop outside Bandar Abbas at early dawn. The air is warm, salt. Make a beeline south to the waterfront on the Persian Gulf. The sun is rising on my left and to the right is the city. The tide is out, leaving little mirrors in the dark sand like tiger skin rippling out toward the sea. There is a little spot out there that looks like a fine place to have a sunrise breakfast before the beach is washed away by the tide.

25

ASIDE: DEAR COAT

Dear coat,

You have hung off my shoulders, worn and torn, but kept me warm through many Scandinavian winters. It was a joy to find you again in a box in the attic, to shrug you on, and hang the backpack over it. Waiting for the train in the Bucharest blizzard would have been terrible without you. You were an appreciated extra blanket in the Cappadocian cave. A familiar weight over my shoulders when they were tense against the desert nights while waiting for buses in Iran.

But this is where we must go on separate adventures. I am going to warm countries now and I cannot carry you with me.

Now that we have travelled east together through old Miklagård, you deserved a flaming Viking longship in the night. You deserved a burial at sea, but you are 60% polyester, and it would be grossly irresponsible to throw you into the ocean. (Though the Persian Gulf is no place to worry about putting petroleum materials into the sea.)

You are staying here now, dear coat, with the nice man who shared his breakfast with us this morning. He was generous, and I am sure he will take care of you.

Enjoy your adventures in Iran. I will enjoy mine further east.

26

A WORD OF WARNING

BANDAR ABBAS, IRAN

Here is a tip if you plan to go by boat between Iran and Dubai! There is a ferry from Bandar Abbas, across to Sharjah in the United Arab Emirate, and from there you can take a bus to Dubai! Cool! However, take a taxi to the harbour. Do *not* attempt to walk from the ticket office in Bandar Abbas to the ferry. Take that taxi. The walk from the bus terminal into town is a nice walk along the beach for a few kilo meters, but the walk from Bandar Abbas to the ferry at Bahonar port is a hell march of about twelve kilometres. The sun is angry and high in the sky. There is no shade for three hours. The ground is mostly broken-up pavement, wet beach sand, gravel, chunks of stone and odd backstreets.

It is reasonable to think that the port is on the coast and that you can just follow the beach to get there, but it is not walkable for long stretches. When you have to start making your way inland, everyone you ask about "Bahonar port to Dubai?" will point you north to the Bahonar *air*-port. They are not the same place.

If you ask for *Bahonar qayak* ("boat," I hope) everyone tells you that it is about five kilometres down the road. During the following hour you lose every gram of salt in your system. It oozes out through your skin and cakes with sweat and road dust whirled up by a thousand heavy trucks passing by (and a thousand merry navy men waving from motorcycles). Your only fortune is that it is mid-February and not a single day closer to summer's heat. Expect to spend more on water along the way than on the taxi that could have saved you from this experience in the first place.

Something in the waterline is rotting and the smell is enough to justify crossing a six-lane motorway to get further away from it. A man selling oranges may take pity on the quixotic moron with the backpack. He may throw you the best orange of your life, free of charge. (I suspect the entertainment was payment enough.) The next truck along the road sells bronze statues of horses. (I would have declined, if offered a free sample. Sorry Mum, no bronze horse.)

HERE IS AN INTERESTING FACT: Bahonar is not only a trade port! Bahonar is also Iran's main naval base, locking the Hormuz Strait. Most internet search results turn out to be images from US military satellites. Are you lost here? On the verge of giving up? Need to ask someone for directions to the Dubai ferry?

Try this:

- approach an armed military barricade
- at Iran's main naval base
- wearing a clearly foreign face
- and carry a big, black backpack

A man with an imposing moustache, black uniform, a fistful of rank stars on his shoulders and mirror shades may take amused pity on you and scribble a note in Farsi. The first part is for a taxi driver (price pre-bargained and underlined twice) and the second part is help to find the terminal. He may shake your hand, wish you welcome to Iran, and then laugh heartily at your idiot ass behind your back as you walk away.

The first part of the note is useless. No one drives an empty taxi this far out. This is the only place in Asia where taxi drivers ignore you instead of honking and stopping on the highway.

You have to walk the last kilometre to the port and start showing the second part of the note to people, like a permission slip from a school nurse. Your face is sunburnt enough that smiling feels strangely stiff, but there is no reason to smile anyway.

At the ticket counter at the port, the clerk raises an eyebrow and ask if you are aware that you are *six hours* early to the ferry, but that is none of his goddamn business.

27

TOWER TO TOWER

BANDAR ABBAS, IRAN TO DUBAI, UNITED ARAB EMIRATES

The night is warm, even out here at sea. The Sharjah/Dubai ferry rumbles across the Persian Gulf in the dark. A flickering TV shows kids' programs over the low murmur of conversation on this sleepless crossing. It is warm and damp, and the seats do not recline quite as much as they should. The Sharjah skyline on the United Arab Emirates side is still invisible on the far side.

Luis, a Spanish TV producer driving from Madrid to Dubai to meet his girlfriend, provides a dinner of bread and sausage for two.

Hours of black water left to cross. Sometime during the night, we pass close enough to Oman's telecom network antennas to receive PriceInfo texts. The gentlemen who run the cafeteria also run a currency exchange service, and with it comes the sobering experience of handing over 350.000 Iranian rials and receiving a handful of spare change. I guess I could buy a cup of coffee or something.

~

Hotel shower. A second skin of dust, grime, dirt and salt washes off into the bathroom drain. I think I am moulting. My skin is visibly paler now.

I had a shower three days ago in Shiraz, where the shower head fell out of the wall and left only a weak trickle from a sad piece of piping. Then: the night bus down to the Gulf coast, followed by several hours of walking up and down streets in Bandar Abbas to find the ticket office for the Valfajr ferry to Sharjah and then the Hell March to said ferry. Then: across the Gulf, curled up on a seat that has seen better days, in moist and tepid air that clung to clothes – air that was only marginally improved in the dry morning heat of the customs office of the United Arab Emirates in Sharjah. After that: another couple of hours waiting in plastic chairs inside a low building in the harbour, while getting a visa processed.

Finally, this (probably stinking) traveller can slide into an air-conditioned taxi that really has not deserved the ill fate of having this (most definitely stinking) traveller on its leather seats.

It is a mercifully short drive from Sharjah to the Naif district of Dubai, where I add one final layer of yuck to my skin by doing comparative hotel-shopping for somewhere to stay. I think I have those cartoon stink lines around me.

I HAVE BEEN in Dubai once before. A couple of years ago a work conference was announced to a secret destination, and with a short packing list: "bring no luggage". Late in the evening, we boarded an airplane whose destination was displayed only as SK7010 UNKNOWN on the departure tables all over the airport. Just after midnight: "this is the captain speaking, you can sleep now". I woke up once during the night to see orange spots of warm light in the black below. Pilot flames from oil towers on Saudi oilfields? The following morning, we landed in a yellow sandscape, disembarked confusedly into dry air and all signs in the small airport were in Arabic. I still savour the feeling of being so utterly lost. The license plates on buses finally gave away our location, and that night all three hundred of us slept on carpets in the desert under perfect starlight.

This time, I am alone in a hotel in the Naif district, but this time Dubai is no fun. Naif is outside the luxury tourist sphere, out where there is trade and nothing else. Dinner: a Coke and a Kit-Kat from a vending machine, because there is nowhere to buy food here, because every single shop in this area is "Wholesale and Export Only". There is something *off* about these shops... Oh, yeah, they stock only one single item of each product, one product sample. Every single piece of property along the streets is a shop not selling its merchandise. It is not until midnight that I find a small shop that actually sells things. I compose another nutritious snack from another bottle of Coke, another Kit-Kat and another bag of chips.

It is impossible to get into Dubai proper from here without a vehicle because there are no footbridges to cross the canals. Gold and jewellery is sold to tourists who are clearly not like me. There is a hole-in-the-wall store in the Gold Souk that sells knock-off brand belt buckles under a LED sign with the slogan "Look Rich". A bitter taste of *I am better than you* because unlike *you* I am a *real* traveller, and that attitude is venomous. They are here to relax; I carry a sense of arrogant, false purity.

I CANNOT REMEMBER GOING to bed, but I wake up and it is dark outside. My circadian rhythm is off, so I might as well finish what I started. A month ago, a train left Stockholm, rolling past the City Hall's red brick tower, through Scandinavia, through Bohemia and Moravia, through Carpathia, Thracia, Anatolia, Persia and across dark water to bright Arabia.

Suffer the final ten kilometres on foot along dark streets and under blinking neon lights, to the impossibly tall Burj Khalifa tower. Its black-and-white line looks like an error on the horizon. After an hour's approach it suddenly shoots up to neck-craning heights.

By fantastical chance, I arrive just in time for the daily closing ceremony, a fountain show on the glittering pool out front set to *Con té partiro*. The fountains, the cool evening air, the paralysing sense of completion. It is impossibly well-timed to arrive right now;

almost choreographed. To arrive at the Burj Khalifa tower exactly one month after I left Stockholm City Hall's brick tower, almost to the hour, tower to tower.

Such an arrival calls for ritual observance. I text my parents and head into the Dubai Mall for the most dignified celebratory dinner I can imagine: a plus-sized McDonald's value meal.

PART III

WILD WILD EAST

Dubai International Airport has over a hundred airlines flying in and out to interesting destinations. How about S7 Airlines to Novosibirsk? RwandAir to Kigali? Kyrgizstan Aircompany? Libyan "Temporarily Suspended" Airlines? Jupiter Airlines straight into Basra, Iraq? C'mon, let's change the plan!

Focus first: Lahore or not? I have a booked hotel and arranged a guide. It would be ridiculous not to go. But the taxi driver said "Lahore BOOM"...

I want to trace the southern fork of the Hippie Trail into western Pakistan, but the situation in Baluchistan has deteriorated. A flight across is necessary. I email the tour operator and ask for advice. "Welcome to the land of colour and culture," "can do the tour without any issue," "Mr. Shahid will meet you at the airport".

I book the flight. DXB to LHE, tonight. Tell Mr. Shahid that I look forward to meeting him.

Next, I text a friend that I am leaving for Lahore. He replies that he will arrange "alternative biomass" for my funeral if they can not scrape together enough of my remains. I'm gonna make new friends when I return home.

28

A ROOM WAITING FOR YOU

DUBAI, UNITED ARAB EMIRATES TO LAHORE, PAKISTAN

The plane crosses back over the Persian Gulf, skirts around the southeast corner of Iran and glides out across a red plain. Ten kilometres below, obscure Baluchistan unfurls with all its Middle East + Wild West trappings: desert, local governance, deep mistrust of the government, arms factories, tribal rule and geopolitics.

The Airbus makes its final approach into after-dark Allama Iqbal International Airport just east of Lahore. In those last few seconds where the plane must push itself down back onto the runway, a hundred cell phones light up. Emirate SIM cards are swapped for Pakistani ones, and the cabin is filled with chirping text messages and outgoing phone calls. "Please ensure that your mobile devices other portable electronic devices remain off until doors are open". Hah.

The arrival hall is chaos. Hundreds are waiting for Pakistani guest workers coming back from Dubai, returning family and international business, and hopefully someone is waiting for me. Cheering, jostling, a gauntlet between cordons that separate the waiting from the arriving, before we can spill out into the hall. No, can not get out that way, too many people. It is a mosh pit now. I find another way back, around and out. The arrival hall floor is strewn with flowers.

I skulk around looking for the taxi driver holding a sign with my name on it, but find no-one. I stay in a holding pattern, walk back and forth, zigzag out onto the parking lot searching, but nothing. What the hell do I do if I can't reach my guide? I collect myself, figure out how to dial the country code, call Mr. Shahid. With every signal I hope hope hope that he will pick up. I take another lap around the arrivals area, declining taxi services by explaining that I'm waiting for a taxi already... but am I?

On the second nervous call, Mr. Shahid does pick up, cheerfully apologising for the misunderstanding. The car is waiting over there, a driver in a blue car to whisk me away along the dark highway towards Lahore, through armed roadblocks and little parks, down Mall Road, past Lahore Zoo and finally pull up outside an, uh, what is this? A Best Western?

A porter in classical uniform insists on carrying my backpack as we duck through a metal detector gate past a rifle-wielding security guard, into an elegant lobby where Mr. Shahid jumps up from a leather couch, beaming, welcoming. When do we start tomorrow, sir? Splendid! I will pick you up outside at eight, then!

Imagine me, who for the last month has slept in train bunks, in Romanian dorms, buses, a cold bed in an Iranian courtyard, folded up on a misty ferry. Fighting exhaustion as the porter brings my bag up to the fourth floor, swipes the keycard, opens the door and wishes me a good night's sleep. Queen-sized bed, marble floor, drapes, a desk, shimmering drapes. There must have been a mix-up. This cannot be my room.

29

LAHORE HERSELF

LAHORE, PAKISTAN

Part the curtains. Behind them is a full-height fourth-floor window overlooking the Mozang district in Lahore, the old Anarkali bazaar and the Qurtaba chowk, where a CIA contractor killed two Pakistani men a few years ago, and caused a diplomatic crisis involving what looks like contract murder, fake license plates, a failed extraction attempt and enough coincidence to make a movie. A colourful neighbourhood.

There are no guests at the breakfast buffet. The dining hall is silent. I am alone, but tables are set, perhaps waiting for more stable times: mornings with bustle and long lines by the wonderfully generous trays of fruit, coffee, pancakes, yoghurt, steaming bread and spicy lentil curry paired with sweet *halwa* paste. My cutlery clinks in isolation. The waiter waits on me only. Outside: the armed guard by the metal detector's arch. This would look good on film. Am I a war reporter now?

Now people stream down from upstairs and ruin the illusion. This is just a fancy hotel with businessmen having coffee. The guard outside is a nice old man with a white twirly moustache, and the metal detector at the gate is not even turned on.

The Grand Trunk Road which is the backbone of all Hind. For the most part it is shaded, as here, with four lines of trees. ... All castes and kinds of men move here. Look! Brahmins and chumars, bankers and tinkers, barbers and bunnias, pilgrims and potters – all the world going and coming. It is to me as a river from which I am withdrawn like a log after a flood. And truly the Grand Trunk Road is a wonderful spectacle.

— KIM, RUDYARD KIPLING (1901)

Kipling called the Grand Trunk Road "a river of life as nowhere else exists in the world," and it sure is. Running all the way from Kabul in Afghanistan, through the legendary Khyber Pass into Pakistan, through Rawalpindi and through Lahore; it carries itself through the border at Wagah into India, down through Delhi and Kolkata, and all the way across to Bangladesh where it ends up in Chittagong, 2500 kilometres all in all.

If my plans survive first contact with reality, I will travel Grand Trunk Road from Lahore to Amritsar and onwards to Delhi. Here, in Lahore, it dissolves into a tangle of streets that Mr. Shahid's driver navigates while I gawk at traffic: trucks, cars, donkey carts, mopeds, handcarts, bicycles, tangles of electrical wire, piles of fruit, horses, decorated buses, motorised rickshaws, chickens and children.

We take a second breakfast in Food Street, cooked in a great iron pan over gas fire in a hole in the wall. Another helping of spicy and sweet out of a bucket. Oh darn, that's right, I still have not sorted out my Hepatitis A yet. Hep A, a disease that is perfectly adapted to spreading through this kind of breakfast service: bucket, sooted iron, plates scrubbed in murky dishwater from a zinc pail.

> usually spread by infected food or water – resistant to detergent and acid – symptoms typically last eight weeks – vomiting – yellow skin – acute liver failure.

But, help me, it is too good. Goddammit.

~

THERE IS something to see around every corner. In-between the classical sights of mosques and Mughal forts are courtyards, labyrinths, markets selling spice by the mound, horses, electrical wiring like cobwebbed trees.

We lose ourselves in the Walled City, the ancient core of Lahore where narrow passages spill into unexpected backyards.

We ascend the wide, flat stairs into the Lahore fort, a royal entrance built for elephants striding up with princes and princesses showered in flower petals from balconies above.

We look over the many domed towers and walls that recede into the red smog over Lahore and we hide from the pale sun in white marble halls, off to the side of a yellowing lawn grown on the top floor of the fort.

We stare in wonder at glittering floral tile decorations in the corridor to emperor Jahangir's tomb, a white marble crypt so opulent I hardly dare touch the walls. The long corridors of the Badshahi mosque where daylight spills in at the far end.

We descend the paradise garden of Shalimar, naked February fruit trees on the terraces where over four hundred fountains wait for the difficult summer heat. Look down into a fountain pit where the walls hold hundreds of little lamps that project rainbows in the mist.

We exit Lahore through the Delhi gate which leads back onto Grand Trunk Road, onwards to India and the Lahore Gate in Delhi.

30

ASIDE: CARD RETAINED

Back in my *real* life, I rely on a debit card and rarely carry cash, but moving around like this means that paper money is king, because (as it turns out) the guy selling fruit from a wooden crate by the highway bus stop at midnight does not take VISA. (Who knew?) There was Damon missing a single Euro coin at the midnight Turkish border crossing, and all of Iran under international banking embargo, and chasing down an exchange office in Bandar Abbas to get hold of some Emirati dirham bills before getting on the boat.

I not have learned my lesson, however. I keep putting off securing paper money until the absolute last theoretical moment. In this case: flying into Pakistan with zero units of Pakistani money because they have ATM:s, right? And of course, they do, Standard Chartered banks all over. I ask the hotel front desk if there is a cash machine nearby and stalk out onto the night streets of Mozang looking for money (a sensible way to behave).

But, um. Tiny problem. My card is not accepted by the ATMs. Hm. Mr. Shahid takes me to a proper bank office that has a proper set of proper ATMs, behind properly lockable doors. But, um. Tiny problem. CARD RETAINED PLEASE CONTACT BRANCH OFFICE, it says. The ATM ate my card. *Shit shit shit.*

With a *slightly* raised pulse I walk into the bank and explain my problem. No worries! I can get it back in just a couple of days. But, um. Tiny problem. I leave Pakistan tomorrow.

They solve it. A security guard is summoned, and I am seated with the branch manager. She has tea served while I wait. I hand over passport. She asks for my story, and counters with her own story: she was brought here from Islamabad to replace a colleague who had, um, tiny problem. I do not ask.

Ah, here is the card (the *relief* of seeing the little orange rectangle in the guard's hand!). Please sign here, and here, in a leather-bound ledger with hundreds of complaints, signed and dated). Thank you so very much, have a nice journey, good day to you!

This does not solve the problem, however. I still need to settle my hotel bill, in cash, so I guess I will just have to keep tryi- CARD RETAINED PLEASE CONTACT BRANCH OFFICE *shit shit shit*

31

BORDER CLOSING CEREMONY

WAGAH, PAKISTAN

Back home in real life, we kept up the Sunday brunches of university life. We still crash on each others' couches and wish for extended weekends and other mercies over tea and scones. On one of those Sundays we saw something incredible on YouTube. We saw the extravagant military ceremony of closing the Wagah border station between Pakistan and India at sunset. We admired border soldiers in parade uniforms, turbans and moustaches. Goose-stepping, hoisting flags, squaring off against others, marching on the verge of dancing, and finishing with a violent handshake across the border. We laughed, we marvelled and we bounced out of the couch to re-enact the stepping stomp, the aggressive handshake, the snapped salute.

In the following years, this border ceremony kept coming up in conversation, in bucket lists, in let-me-show-you-somethings. I wanted to see it. I had to see it. I had to go there one day. I had to travel to that border station. Now, finally, that border station is just a few kilometres from here, just east of Lahore.

Michael Palin calls it "carefully choreographed contempt"; this daily 30-minute showdown where Pakistani and Indian border rangers lower their flags and close the border where the Grand Trunk Road crosses from Pakistani Lahore on this side over to Indian Amritsar on that side. It is designed to ritually calm tensions on the border, so the ceremony is carefully mirrored across the Radcliffe line. Soldiers on either side collaborate to put on a spectacular show for the massive crowds that come up from Pakistan and India to cheer for their "team". Ah, one side will stretch their kicks a bit higher, and one side will keep their flag hoisted for a half-second longer than the suckers on the other side. A spectacular show it is.

We drive the Grand Trunk Road up towards Wagah, and Mr. Shahid negotiates seats that are usually not available. Good friends with some of the rangers, apparently. I approach the red brick arch over the single road link into India and it looks just like in the video we saw on the couch years ago, because *it is*. It is crisper, paler, fragrant, bright. It is 360 all around me; I can stomp the asphalt myself. *This is it.* I've made it.

Birdsong gives way to patriotic Pakistani pop and we take our seats. The afternoon sun glints in golden ornaments on the border gate. A white-bearded man with the name MC Imran embroidered across his back works up the audience. On the Indian side of the border, a much larger Indian crowd take their seats while their master of ceremony whip up thunderous applause. A kid loses her balloon. It floats upwards until it is just a small dot on the pale sky and it will likely be an illegal immigrant to India within minutes.

A group of school girls in purple uniform are led to their seats by their teacher. Green Pakistani flags are sold along with drinks and snacks. One single bus carries travellers from India into Pakistan just after the official closing time. It is the Sada-e Sarhad bus, the only road vehicle allowed to cross this border. Established as a way to let families separated by the Partition of India and Pakistan to visit each other, it remains an important part of de-escalating tensions on either side. A horn is blown and then everything happens.

I recognise the drum rhythm from that Youtube Sunday. The rangers stomp up to the gate, stepping and kicking. They march up and down the courtyard, stomp and shout, turn and power-pose. They bang the gate, lower the flag and I'm *sure* we won. They fold it up, snap out the handshake and salute and carry away the flag on outstretched arms like a ceremonial pillow and it's all wonderfully complete and it is all I thought it would be. It is a surreal ceremony, and surreal to have sat on a couch and seen something on Youtube and surreal to actually be here to see the black-dressed soldiers and their fanned turbans rush the flag to bed. Surreal, this: to make myself a promise and to roll up to the border in a Mr. Shahid's BMW years later.

To Mr. Shahid over the music: I'M ACTUALLY HERE! but I don't think he gets it.

32

A (VACCINATION) PLAN COMES TOGETHER

LAHORE, PAKISTAN

I somehow neglected getting my Hepatitis A shots before I left. It got lost in all the hauling-stuff-into-storage and saying-goodbye-to-people. No biggie, I could have fixed it in Copenhagen. But then I passed through Copenhagen well before sunrise. Then I stayed in Berlin just for a few hours. And then, Carpathian countryside. Vaccination did not happen.

Istanbul? Missed the train, got to stay in a major capital for a few days. Plenty of time to visit a few landmarks, decompress in a hostel, find a doctor, get needled, no problem... but after being turned down in three different clinics, I became concerned.

A fellow backpacker at my hostel put me in contact with one of her friends in Tehran, who in turn booked a visit to a vaccination clinic, and her boyfriend offered to drive me there, but a week later, I learned that Iran does not provide Hep A shots at all.

A friend back home relayed of her contacts: an actual doctor, in actual Lahore. A humble email: would it be possible to find Havrix or something like that in Lahore on short notice? A quick reply: he has contacted his supervisor, who just happens to be an international expert in clinical immunology. She, in turn, arranges for a doctor to come straight to my hotel room to get this done. First rule of going to India without a Hep A shot is to not go to India without a Hep A shot.

But, um, I'm crossing into India, like, tomorrow, so, um, if it isn't too much trouble, could you, um, I hate to ask, come here before lunch? The border at Wagah closes at 3 o'clock sharp, and there's customs to take care of and the drive up to the border can get... oh, OK. Thank you so much.

Bags packed. The doctor will be here at 11, Mr. Shahid will pick me up at 12, I cross the border well before closing time. All is well. I ask the reception if I can stay in the room for a while past the checkout time? I'm, uh, expecting a visit. From a doctor.

Time ticks past 11.00, and then 11.30. No doctor yet. He is stuck in traffic. No worry. This will be quick. Mr. Shahid arrives to take me up to the border and I have to explain that we just need to wait a little. Ahem. 12.30. Sorry to cause trouble. 12.35. Time is running out. Phone call! The vaccinator has conquered the traffic jam only to arrive at the wrong Best Western in Lahore. Time just ran out. Sigh. I wonder if I can get vaccinated at the customs office...

But Mr. Shahid, this organising angel, snatches the phone out of my hand and makes an arrangement to meet "somewhere along the way". We pile into the car and head back out on Mall Road, out towards the Indian border. We have little more than two hours to get through traffic, converge with the good doctor, race out of Lahore and up to Wagah, and get through customs. Perhaps we should just give up and book the hotel for another night?

An "arrangement to meet along the way" is how I ended up getting vaccinated in the backseat of a car in a dusty parking lot in Pakistan, with a doctor who just appeared out of nowhere on a scooter, with a shot of Havrix and a syringe packed up in a plastic bag wrapped around the handle. No payment, Sir! No cost!

Three minutes flat, and then we are back on the Grand Trunk Road, speeding toward the border.

My vaccination card was unreachable at the bottom of the bag, so I have a vaccination certificate scribbled on a crumpled Post-It note folded into my passport. Let's see if I can get this baby notarised when I get home. I have certainly been enough trouble in this country already.

33

DISPUTED BORDER

LAHORE, PAKISTAN TO AMRITSAR, INDIA

Next challenge: actually *crossing* the infamous India-Pakistan border! Carved out of the Kashmir during the partition of Pakistan from India, it runs along the Radcliffe Line, named after Sir Cyril Radcliffe who designed the partition of Pakistan from India; it was he who drew the line. The Wikipedia article has an entire sub-section on "Problems in the process" and a sub-sub-section on "Haste and indifference":

> All lawyers by trade, Radcliffe and the other commissioners had all of the polish and none of the specialised knowledge needed for the task. They had no advisers to inform them of the well-established procedures and information needed to draw a boundary. Nor was there time to gather the survey and regional information.
>
> — RADCLIFFE LINE, WIKIPEDIA

Radcliffe himself had never been to India and had no contact network in Asia – perfectly impartial to both India and to the newly formed state (but of course, partial to old Britain). The division turned out *so-so* with many unresolved consequences that may never be explained, especially since Radcliffe destroyed all records and documentation on the process before leaving India. The results of the division have caused a long and bloody conflict along what The Economist calls "the world's most dangerous border".

No more than thirty minutes before the single crossing on that border closes, we arrive at Wagah/Attari station. I say goodbye to Mr. Shahid, shrug on my backpack and attempt to walk out of Pakistan. Birds can still be heard as the border ceremony has not started yet. This is going to be interesting, potentially difficult and at the very least an adventure. But there is no-one here.

I try an open door into a customs building; air-conditioned, dark, empty. Spill out onto sunny asphalt on the far side, follow a sign toward the actual gate out into the zone between the borders. Armed guards by a garden table, a huge ledger, a cup filled with pens. A quick look at my passport. I am signed in with date, name and nationality, by hand, in ballpoint pen. I recognise the system from somewhere else:

> ...all eight of us would pile out of our vehicles and write down every last detail of our passports and prolix visas in a book the size of a tabletop, a process that would take up to half an hour each time. After the first dozen or so, it became apparent that nobody would notice if I just wrote in whatever popped into my head, which made the wait slightly more entertaining.
>
> I like to imagine that somewhere in Pakistan there is a giant warehouse being filled with these books, like the treasure repository in Indiana Jones. One day in the future, I imagine, a bored security guard will decide to open a register at random, and as he's leafing through the pages, his eyes will fall upon a barely legible scrawl indicating that on December 8th, 2011, a young man from Memphis named Elvis Presley passed through several checkpoints in the wastes of Balochistan.
>
> — THE PAKISTAN CHRONICLES, ADAM HODGE

Here comes the moment of truth, at this worn plastic table, in the company of Pakistani border guards with real guns. If this turns out to be an impasse, I am stuck. I have no other idea of how to get out of Pakistan, much less how to reach Kathmandu. I would have to return to Lahore somehow, extend the hotel stay without any cash, book a flight from Allama Iqbal to... where? The oven-hot courtyard between orange brick walls and arches is empty, except for us. The Pakistani and Indian flags are hoisted just to the side, uneasy on a cold wind.

I write my name as legibly as I can, projecting a polite? humble? trustworthy? body language, bent over the ledger. This absolutely needs to work; I *must* succeed in crossing here. Will it look suspiciously rehearsed if I write down my passport number from memory? It is silly, but I pretend to read it off the page.

After I have registered my exit, I leave the guards at the table and walk the final stretch up to the gate out of Pakistan. I am extremely self-conscious of just how I should approach and hand over my passport to the last guard; the final boss. He inspects the photo page. He flips through every page, past a wide collection of stamps and visas. He studies the little pasted-in Pakistani visa that required so much work to get. When he starts flipping through the pages a second time, a surge of adrenalin. "Sir," he says, "there is no exit stamp?"

I am kindly turned back to get my passport marked up properly. Explain to the curious guards at their garden table why I am coming back into Pakistan again.

In the customs building, I finally find someone and explain that I need an, uh, "exit stamp"? He summons a group of officers who turn on a computer, gather around scan my passport, declare an, ah, computer problem. Please fill out this form. I fill out the form with a pen the documentary film maker gave me on the ferry back in Denmark. A nice pen, apparently, since the officer asks if he can keep it please? (So, David, your pen is now an instrument of the Pakistani government.)

Thank you and welcome back in Pakistan, sir!

I pass through the iron gate into the absolutely silent zone between the two states. I am the only passenger on a colourful, decked-out, straight-up *bling* shuttle bus to the Indian side.

The "IN-PAK border is impossible to cross," but I was seconds from walking out of Pakistan illegally.

34
KEYS
ATTARI, INDIA

The iron gates out from Pakistan shut behind me, and the shuttle bus's door closes. The shuttle follows a little asphalt road across a field towards the Indian customs building, through a roundabout and past low, long buildings. The bus rattles and tinkles with little bells and pearls and chimes. I hang briefly between two nations' border stations. No plans ahead of me, no phone reception and no-one waiting for me anywhere. No other passengers. Apart from driver and guard, I am alone between chain link fences and barbed wire. An eerie place to feel such intense freedom, but I absorb it; try to hold on to it.

The Indian visa on page 15 of my passport is the key that will hopefully unlock the gate in that sand-yellow building and carry me onto the Grand Trunk Road again, down the Punjab plain, through Amritsar and on down to Delhi, Sunauli, Kathmandu.

A thought: *I have no keys*. Strange, because I have always had key rings gnawing holes in my pockets. Cannot remember when I got my own keys to our apartment as a child, but I do remember how my friend and I shared a padlocked school locker and wired up a battery-driven alarm bell with a tin-foil trigger to keep the locker "extra safe". Keys and codes carved out a small volume of space accessible only to us.

More fences and barbed wire cross the field. I think I am technically in India now. Hard to tell – there is not a no-man's-land zone here; the countries run right up to each other. The bus pulls up with a heavy sigh outside the customs building. My bag is x-rayed on a little conveyor belt, and I step through a metal detector archway. I have no keys to put in the little plastic tray.

I have always owned keys, and always got the next set of keys before the old ones were handed in. Keys to club storage, to a locker, to a safe, padlock, work, home, cupboards. Something to prove access rights to somewhere. Jagged metal teeth fill the missing pieces of the tumbler lock puzzle on apartment doors; curled-up radio antennas in key fobs sing a secret radio melody to electronic locks; magnetic strips on swipe cards stutter out the correct rhythm to magstripe locks.

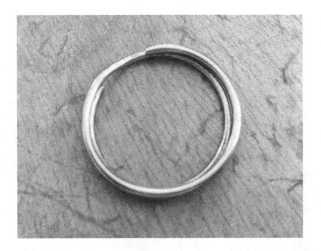

Now: no apartment keys, I don't have a home. No storage keys, they are locked up in an attic. No attic keys, they are with Dad. No key cards or key fobs. With the last little padlock key handed off to Dad at the train station in Stockholm, there is no longer any indoor volume in the world that is private to me.

The bag is x-rayed once more; a customs officer opens every single zippered compartment to inspect its contents. Leafs through my India guidebook. Finally, I walk out onto Indian asphalt and hop into a rickety mini-van that rolls down the plateau towards Amritsar.

The van is protected from theft by a padlock bolted to the door.

35

MULTI SUPER LUXURY LEADER

AMRITSAR, INDIA

For the sake of symmetry, the driver pulls up just outside the Lahori gate in Amritsar, and I am immediately lost in dusty alleys that fill the spaces inside the city walls. Somewhere in this tangle is the Golden Temple of Amritsar, a peaceful place behind white walls with a gold foil-covered sanctum on a pool of cool water where dipping swollen feet is encouraged.

The map only shows the larger threads in this web of alleys, so it is impossible to get any sense of scale. Hard to know if I am halfway to the central temple or if I already missed it and should be heading back. The way "back" was lost long ago, for that matter. I have no sense of direction down here at the bottom of the Menger sponge that is Amritsar's old town. But I asked for this. I just love getting lost in new cities, don't I? Best way to get to know the neighbourhood, right..?

No line of sight is longer than a few meters on these twisting streets. They are all cut short by buildings or tottering donkey-carts loaded with swaying stacks of bales. Impossible to know if I am even going toward the centre.

Knees ache under my backpack, calves and thighs tingle slightly from not eating enough. I could stop and buy something to eat from the little shops on either side, but I am oddly reluctant to break stride... or to negotiate a purchase without any language skills. No sense of progress through this labyrinth. The sky is a milky yellow, unwilling to share even the direction of the sun for navigation.

The pompous advertisements of Asia: a scuffed and dusty truck is the "leader in cash logistics." A rundown apartment on the second floor that has laundry and electrical cabling pouring out the window is a "Multi Super Burn Unit Hospital". I would not take a paper-cut up there, and that is coming from someone who had an injection in a parking lot just this morning.

(Am I heckling a hospital for their marketing now? I need to eat and sleep. This has been a difficult day.)

It is clear that I am not going to figure out the Golden Temple thing today. It is around here somewhere, but I am done; spent. I have to stop walking without a plan, sit down on a bed, get some carbohydrates and lose consciousness on a soft pillow. That's it.

On a corner, a hotel with prices just under the small amount of cash rupees I have. The sign by the door says "Luxury". It will do. Sign name into a big ledger. A spiral staircase that just fits my backpack leads up far more turns than my knees agreed to, but lookie here: a penthouse studio with a terrace! (It is a cell with a shared sink out on the roof.) Pale light filters through wooden blinds. My peripheral vision is flickering from exhaustion, but I am somehow to buzzed to wind down. Might be hunger, might be crisis. Sit on the bed, too tired to unlace my boots. Restless. Pace back and out on the terrace. Look down in the street. Loose bricks and AC units hanging outside windows by their last bolt.

Lie on the bed. Flip through the guidebook. No mention of Amritsar at all.

Still weirdly wound up. The colours outside the blinds shift. An hour's uneasy rest, and then slink back out in the streets in the afternoon heat. A couple of laps around the building, careful not to lose track of the hotel. Too exhausted to attempt finding, understanding and navigating a proper restaurant, especially not knowing the purchasing power of the little cash I have left. Settle for yet another bag of chips and a dusty bottle of Coke that has been on the shelf since the Mughal empire, at an unknown currency exchange rate.

The door to my room doesn't stay closed when shut, so I lean the bag on it to keep it in place while I sleep, lulled by noises and voices from the narrow street below.

I wake up again at dusk. One of the temple spires is right outside the window, lavender in the sunset.

36

THOMAS WAS ALONE

AMRITSAR, INDIA

In the game "Thomas Was Alone," a red rectangle named Thomas suddenly comes into existence, and realises he is alone in the world. Thomas finds his way upwards and to the right by climbing, jumping and solving puzzles.

They say solo travelling is not lonely. They say you *depart* alone, but *travel* with newfound friends. Come to think of it, I have not spent many days' time alone on the way here, if any. But up here at the top of a spiral staircase in north-western India, after little more than a month of travelling, suddenly loneliness is crushing. No warning.

"The loneliness was getting to Thomas. No amount of observation or obsessive note taking could combat that."

They say India is a challenging place to travel. The intensity, the size, the poverty, the chaos, the traffic, the transport, the totality of the experience. In this I have no plan, no language, no experience, no communications, no currency; and crucially, no energy to fix any of the above.

I work slowly, one small step at a time. Short trips down the stairs and out the door. Find an ATM. Return to my room.

Find something to eat. Find a little lawn. Return to my room. Find the entrance to the temple. Good work. Return to my room.

Find an internet café close to the temple. Find something to cover my head with. Find my way around the temple complex. Find the peace to walk into the temple and find my way around the pool and the golden house at its centre. Find the time to just sit down for a while.

The sky is lavender again, the water is lapping at the edge of the sacred pool and people keep making steady clockwise laps around it. I am in no hurry. I can sit right here until everything feels fine gain.

An hour.

Three hours.

Really, I could stay here for weeks if I wanted to.

I have nowhere to be.

My schedule; my pace.

They say that the Golden Temple is a place where you can stay and eat for free in a dormitory that is a part of the complex in exchange for volunteering in the kitchen. They say that it is something you simply must do, if you can figure out how. So, let's take that leap. Get the bag from the hotel, get back out there and hope to figure out how to get a bed at the Sri Guru Ram Das Niwas before dark. More walking. Everywhere, tout calls: *taxi for Wagah border ceremony!* No thanks, I just came from there. OK, sir, OK. *Taaaxi for Wagah border!*

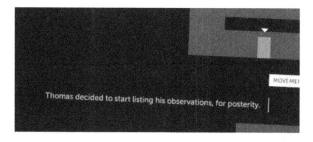

"*Thomas decided to start listing his observations, for posterity.*"

They say to ask for assistance, help. To muster up the energy to ask someone. Damn. It was never this hard to ask for directions. But yes, the dormitories are just opposite the eastern gate to the Golden Temple. Just have to ask by the little counter, then apply with the old Sikh who runs the tourist cells, and be lucky enough that there is a free bed, and wait around in the courtyard. And... bingo.

Harmandir Sahib, the golden temple, is one of the holiest places in Sikhism. The four gates to the temple grounds are open to the north, east, south and west to welcome people from all parts of the world, offering food and rest to those who need it. The temple kitchen provides free meals in a frantic mass-production facility where hundreds of volunteers bake bread, hundreds chop onions and hundreds do the dishes for the benefit of helping out. Tens of thousands eat here, every day, all year around. Around the clock, every day, people come here to get their hands dirty and/or their stomachs filled. Contribute money or contribute labour or contribute both, or neither, but anyone can line up for a hot meal and a bowl of milky chai.

~

THE COMING DAYS ARE RECUPERATION. Good sleep in the temple dormitory shifts into aimless walking around Amritsar's central area in search for breakfast. Long walks looking at things; looking *for* things. Lazy plodding around and around and around the temple pool, a twinkling golden box out in the middle of the water anchoring each barefoot lap. Sit down, look at people. Birds and kites. Back out in the streets again, counter-clockwise this time. Hello Dog, it is me again. Be careful in the streets, will you?

A little later I am in the dish duty line with new friends outside the temple kitchen, scrubbing lentil and onion from a literal thousand plates, in a place that has come to feel just as much home as the hostel in Istanbul, the train station in Kayseri or any apartment in Stockholm ever did.

"*Thomas had a new theory. The world was training him. He could feel himself getting smarter. He was evolving. He just wished he had someone to share it with.*"

37

TEMPLE DAYS

AMRITSAR, INDIA

New friends with dreads, paisley pants and good travel war stories drop into the Ram Das Niwas dormitory at the Golden Temple. Backpackers come streaming past the beds in the dormitory hall, or move in and out of the little adjoined bed-cells that have actual doors. Some turn around and go looking for something else. Some stay. Eric and Cindii (Maltese hippies) stay. James (Australian kid who hitchhiked here from Turkey) stays. Jackie (on the tail end of her India trip) leaves for Delhi to go home. Marco hangs around.

To the temple comes Chataki, British old-school new-age lady in the world's brightest colours. She bounces around the complex with an air of having been to India a dozen times and... oh, she has been here a full dozen times.

We crash out on the side-by-side beds here at the Sri Guru Ram Das Niwas. Rest up. The sky shifts from bright blue to a dusty yellow in the afternoon, and then purple in the evening. Shoes on, shuffle across the road, shoes off, bowl of chai on carpets in the warm night. Walk a few more laps around the pool. Must have walked a hundred laps by now.

The Golden Temple is the literal home of the central text of Sikh faith: Guru Granth Sahib, written by a succession of Gurus. The book itself is the final Guru, and is treated with the same reverence as its ancestors before it, including being carried off to a bed in its own room at night.

The outer walls of the complex are chalk-white in the day. Electric white under floodlights in the evening. Streaks of sweet in the evening air.

The chants have stopped now, and the great book that lives in the golden house has been carried out and tucked into a bed. The air is still filled with birds and kites, some of which have lost their strings and balance on hot air before they dive into the water.

Back on the beds in the dormitory cell, we compare notes and help each other plan our next steps across the subcontinent. There is a big old classroom map of India on the far wall. Don't go to Delhi! Go to Rishikesh; go south to Kerala; go up to the border; go up to Kashmir and Shimla.

We cross the road between the dormitory and the temple barefoot because all of us are hippies now. A couple of midnight laps around the temple pool, then huddle together on carpets with chai bowls in the warm dark. The water on the Sarovar – the "tank of nectar" – around the temple is still. When the temperature drops, we wrap ourselves up in blankets and stay just a little longer. Huddle up under one of the arches on the wide sidewalk around the temple complex; the golden Harmandir Sahib box illuminated by floodlights at its centre. A sparse group of pilgrim and tourist silhouettes still circle around around around the pool. Soft conversations in Hindi and English and Punjabi and Gujarati and Italian and German. Soft sitar over raspy loudspeakers.

∼

THE 30-YEAR ANNIVERSARY of Operation Blue Star is coming up in a few months. In early June 1984, armoured tanks surrounded this temple. Soldiers were stationed on the roofs surrounding it.

The Sikh had been dealt a bad hand by India's independence, squeezed between Hindu-majority India and Muslim Pakistan. Activists had called for a home state: the creation of Israel and Pakistan inspired visions of a similar Sikh nation, Khalistan. A nationalist movement grew, with this Golden Temple as its base. Weapons piled up right here, with the low murmurs, the fading sitar. Hundreds were killed as the army flushed out the extremists who had turned it into a rebel stronghold.

In its attack on the temple, the army was under strict orders not to fire at the golden Harmandir Sahib, and not at the white Akal Takht, bright pastel in noon sunlight. Damaging the Sikhs' holiest temple would be a devastating trigger. Yet, on the third day, artillery and mortars rained shells and grenades into the complex from the surrounding alleys. On the fourth day of the siege, tanks rolled in and shelled the Akal Takht's white walls.

Where now the salty scent of *karah parshad* offerings and wafting masala from the tea tank hangs on the evening air, hung the stench of death in 1984.

38

ASIDE: TO INDIA IN SIX DAYS

Border to border, my passage to India took one month, almost to the day. Between nights curled up on a seat on a train through Slovakia, freezing under thin blankets in Romania, trying to sleep through calls to prayer in Turkey and trekking a dry highway in Iran, it has been an uncomfortable journey thus far.

Still better than the alternatives a century ago – months of travel through deserts and over mountains. Then, the "overland" route by ship cut the time to just weeks.

> the most superb fleets in the world; and the "Overland Route" has been adopted as the most expeditious and regular channel by which Englishmen dispatch their letters and transport themselves from Southampton to the Ganges; and *vice versá*. India, which it formerly took four or five months to reach, is now brought within forty-five days' distance of the mother country.

— THE OVERLAND COMPANION: BEING A GUIDE FOR THE TRAVELLER TO INDIA VIA EGYPT, J. H. STOCQUELER (1850)

Then the 1930's, and commercial air travel happened. Though blindingly expensive, a *flying-boat* would whisk you to far shores in a week or less, with breakfast served in bed.

ENGLAND—EGYPT—INDIA   By *Imperial* flying-boat to Karachi, thence by land-plane to Calcutta.
Beginning Wednesday 5th July, 1939.

Miles from South-ampton	PORTS OF CALL Junctions and Termini are shown in CAPITALS (See notes at foot)	Local Standard Time	Greenwich Mean Time	Days of Services	
				Every	
	LONDON................... dep. Southampton *England*........... tr.	19 30 21 28	18 30 20 28	Sun.	Wed.
624 1005 1325 1704	SOUTHAMPTON............dep. Marseilles *France*............dep. Rome *Italy*....................dep. Brindisi *Italy*.................dep. Athens *Greece*.................arr.	05 00 10 10 13 15 16 00 19 50	04 00 09 10 12 15 15 00 17 50	Mon.	Thur.
2291 2644 3133 3446	Athens.......................dep. ALEXANDRIA *Egypt* (A).....dep. Tiberias* *Palestine*..........dep. Habbaniyeh *Iraq*.............dep. Basra *Iraq*..................arr.	04 30 09 30 12 50 17 10 19 20	02 30 07 30 10 30 14 10 16 20	Tues.	Fri.
3791 4091 4831	Basra.......................dep. Bahrein *off Arabia*...........dep. Dubai *Oman*.................dep. Karachi *India*................arr.	05 00 08 05 11 15 18 50	02 00 04 45 07 25 13 30	Wed.	Sat.
5273 5576 5820 5931 6406	Karachi.....................dep. Jodhpur *India*...............dep. Delhi *India*..................dep. Cawnpore *India*..............dep. Allahabad *India*..............dep. CALCUTTA *India*.............arr.	02 00 05 45 08 55 11 05 12 30 16 31	20 30 00 15 03 25 05 35 07 00 10 37	Thur.	Sun.

— Matt Novak, Paleofuture

Until you see the timetable. Ah, there is the catch: departures at 4 or 5 in the morning for a week. No thanks. By sticking to night buses and a slow itinerary, I have not set a morning alarm for weeks. I'm not changing that for anything.

39

CHANGE OF PLANS

AMRITSAR TO HARIDWAR, INDIA

"Don't go to Delhi man, go to Rishikesh."
We stand in front of the map hanging on the back wall of the dormitory on the temple entrance. I had planned to follow the Grand Trunk Road down to Delhi, through Varanasi and up north to the Nepalese border crossing at Sunauli. Now better travelled people suggest a detour to Rishikesh, the legendary hippie hotspot where the Beatles... did stuff, I suppose? From there, I should be able to head straight to Varanasi and get back on track.

Here is another mistake to avoid: attempting to buy train tickets from the rail company yourself. There is a healthy ecosystem of ticket vendors that book trips for others, but hey, I am in no hurry. I'm a strong, independent backpacker who don't need no middleman. Turns out that those businesses exist for a reason.

Line up. Wait for forty minutes. Indian Railways run their booking system off a text-based computer system. This part of the system is computerised, but there is a worrying number of people filling out forms and papers around the ticket hall. "One ticket to Rishikesh, please!" Hah! Did I think it was that simple? That the people filling out forms did it because they prefer it? Hah! Please fill out this form, sir, and line up again! The pain of having to get out of the line and start over is dulled by the complexity of the form.

Please fill out the train number you want to travel with.

Please fill out the starting and ending stations.

Please fill out "boarding at" ... oh, those were supposed to be the *train's* starting and ending stations? Not the stations I travel between?

The form says "reservation requisition" – it is just an on-paper way to ask if there is a free seat in the exact configuration jotted down. What happens if there is no seat like this? Fill out another form and go back to the line?

If you don't want to avail upgradation scheme, write "No" in box (If this option is not exercised, passengers may be upgraded automatically)

What? Damn this triple negation!

Train name..? That is easy, it is probably somewhere on that huge timetable on the wall. Wait, that table is only for southbound trains; northbound trains are listed somewhere else. Form filled out, back in line... but just as it is my turn to approach the counter again, everything closes down for Indian Railways' synchronised, nationwide tea break.

JUST AS I am about to leave, the rest of the temple dormitory gang show up with newly bought tickets to join me up to Rishikesh. We hop into a motorickshaw and crush its suspension under the weight of our bags. It putters through the crowded night-streets of Amritsar, past brightly lit storefronts and silhouettes of cattle and soon we sprawl out on the platform, on the carpets James carries everywhere, under yellow, insect-swarmed lamps. Train announcements in Hindi are signalled by the *plonk* error sound from Windows 95. We wait.

Tonight again, a train rolls out into the night, slowly enough that barking dogs can chase us through the dark backyards below the railway embankment. Five Sikh brothers share the bench opposite and insist that I give their Punjabi pop an ear-piercing listen. Do you like?

The sleeper car is more of a cattle car: the bunks are rubber-draped benches in the usual three tiers. The windows are prison-barred, and the stagnant air is freezing. I am wearing everything I own, hugging my backpack to hold on to *something*, hood pulled down over my eyes to block out the tube lights in the ceiling, where spinning table fans are mounted a little too close to my toes.

But outside in the absolute dark, long, sad whistle notes from locomotives rise and fall with Doppler shift as we roll toward Uttarakhand state. This is *exactly* what I wanted India to be: dreadlocked hippies and a cocky Australian kid I met two days ago, on an unplanned geographical diversion on a spartan night train into a Himalaya corner I know nothing about.

PART IV

HIMALAYA

A train whistles through misty jungle morning. Going slow enough to lean out of the train car door, breath warm air and squint in the headwind. Broken roads and collapsed bridges peek out between trees. This is the foothills of the Himalayas. Somewhere at the far end of them: Kathmandu's dusty squares and boxy brick temples and prayer bunting flags flapping on the wind.

40

TRAINS AND MOTORICKSHAWS

HARIDWAR TO RISHIKESH, INDIA

A man passes through the cold train, selling hot chai from a steaming tank. A sparse forest in thick mist, thin black lines in the grey. Soft rain pitter-patters on the train roof when it makes halt. Little monkeys on a station platform. Playing chess on James' magnetic travel chessboard, snapping taken pieces to an overhead metal bar. Cindii preaches the gospel of coconut oil as a remedy for everything, specifically the sunburn on my ear from Iran (it does help).

We change trains somewhere. More little monkeys. The mist

smells like something, something other than jet fuel and carpeting. Instead of a refrigerated airplane sandwich, we munch on breakfast samosas bought on the train platform before our next train climbs out of the mist into warm noon.

Disembark in Haridwar, and from here we take a slow motorickshaw downhill to northern Rishikesh. When the haze clears, our world has become a green Himalaya valley cut through by the Ganges' slow winter flow, its mythical source just kilometres north from here.

Dropped off on a steep road on the side of the valley, at the top of an even steeper staircase down towards the water. This is where the river exits the deep mountain valleys and flows out onto the open Gangetic plain. "New Agers go here," says our driver, an eye to Eric's and Cindii's dress and dreads. He gestures across a long suspension bridge across the Ganges.

Thaw out in the warm sand on its banks, accompanied by a sociable buffalo. It is as clingy as a puppy, its muzzle deep in our bags, licking everything.

Above us, pilgrims stream across the Ram Jhula suspension bridge; some seeking the spiritual proximity to the river, and some seeking the spiritual proximity to charlatan ashrams that peddle remedies. Are you aware that today, human intelligence is too focused on remembering things from our, eh, memory banks, so that we recycle thoughts faster and faster, and that this leads to insanity? No? Then join this spiritual class. You will learn how to ride the twelve-year solar cycles; to bring your body into the same cycle as the sun. If your cycle is shorter than three months you will, psychologically, need, um, medical treatment. You can also discover "that which is imprinted as DNA in our innerself," become "able to neutralise unfavourable planetary influences," learn "a way to energise yourself by solar radiation" (also known as vitamin D) and, oh, go bungy jumping.

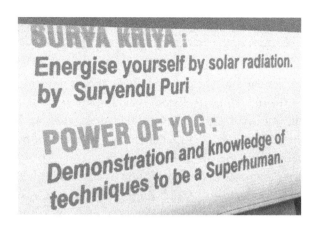

The hippies go off to find a hippie field to pitch their hippie tent. I go off to find a decent bed. Let us meet for dinner later, eh? With the big black back-breaking back-pack chafing my shoulders, I follow a thin, winding strip of asphalt that climbs out of the humid haze down by the river, and up up up through little communities and clusters of ashrams and mega-temples. A sign warns of aggressive monkeys up ahead, then of dogs. Advertisement of yoga classes in specific jargon are plastered across every flat surface.

Up up up, against a river of tourist buses that freewheel down the serpentine road. Lactic burn, and a familiar thirst. I start avoiding hotels on the left side of the road, since their driveways run uphill. After an hour's search, everything is still fully booked, but maybe a room for next week, sir?

A promising alley leads away from the bustle, ever higher up the side. A little way along the alley, discreet, hand-painted signs advertise BnBs and retreats. Small houses dot the sides of the path, a school, a little shop that sells cold water. Balance over planks laid out across a muddy field. Every little BnB advertised is fully booked. I am offered a little backyard shack, but it turns out to be a mistake: the tenants will be back tonight, sir.

It is the very last house at the back of the village, up against the curving incline of the mountain ridge, that has a room. But sir, for two nights! only two nights!

A bed, a water tap, a door and a veranda overlooking the valley I just climbed up. Emerald green everywhere and a hazy blue sky behind the ridge on the far side. All the Himalayan scents of the valley come welling up, borne on warm air: water, earth, flowers, fields, spices. A rickety wooden ladder leads up to the rooftop, and I can not resist climbing to overlook it all. There is a single plastic chair, just for me. Houses, electric blue and cherry pink and snow white, laid out in all the green. It is absolutely silent up here. The air is clear. The bustle of Rishikesh can not be seen nor heard from here. There is only the village and the valley.

I come down again for dinner. A little late. Wait for the others on the dark bridgehead of the Ram Jhula, a suspension bridge blocked by a Very Important Cow that must be pushed aside. Monkeys race back and forth on the railing, but my entourage is nowhere to be found. Without phone numbers, there is precious little to do but patiently wait, like in the bad old days. I walk around for a bit. Talk to a dog. Look at people. Look at food. Go back to wait again. Soon, it is dark.

James shows up eventually, having waited by the northern bridge. The kids are checked into a nice hotel on the main street, paying about half of what I do – but 200% of very little money is still very little money.

At dinner, a man at our table shares a personal story about how he became a ray of pure energy and spoke with Shiva. He explains that humans vibrate at the wrong natural frequency to be able to experience true love. He one-ups the entire flat-earth, moon hoax, truther community by exposing NASA's lies – it is actually *the Moon* which is flat!

~

WE ASCEND AN ABANDONED hotel construction project on the riverbank: four floors of naked concrete stairs and dark floors without walls. From its roof: the expanse of the dark river glittering yellow in the lights of Rishikesh. When we climb down the non-walled staircase again our eyes are fully adjusted to the dark. The floors are crowded with sleeping people rolled up in sleeping bags and mattresses.

Warm rain blankets the street outside; shimmers in the light from little shops and bakeries. Tourists run laughing through the deluge. Thunder booms to the south, white lightning arcs from one side of the valley to the other. James and I head out to look at thunder from the other bridge – the Laxman Jhula – until we realise that a tall metal suspension bridge next to a statue of Shiva the Destroyer is perhaps not the best lookout place during a thunderstorm.

41

BETTING ON A BORDER

RISHIKESH, INDIA

The main border crossing into Nepal is through Sunauli, at the midpoint of India's northern border, a few days east from here. I plan to follow the Ganges southeast, through holy Varanasi and then north across the border, up to Kathmandu, and turn west towards the Annapurna mountain range.

Poor James is going home to start his academic year in Australia and does not have the time to see Nepal. His winding adventure from Turkey, through less travelled parts of Iran, through Baluchistan and Pakistan has brought him so close to Nepal, but he is too late to reach Kathmandu.

No. Wait. There *has* to be a border crossing closer than Sunauli. It must be possible to enter western Nepal from here. The bulk of travellers follow the Delhi-Varanasi-Gorakhpur-Sunauli-Kathmandu route. It has been the main overland trail since the first Intrepid hippies came through here decades ago.

> For the earth bound amongst us it's a bus or truck up from Birgunj, an uncomfortable ride due to the constant twists, turns, ups and downs for over 200 kilometers. If you've ever ridden a see-saw for twelve hours you'll know the feeling. Make sure you get deluxe seats, they ... are within the bus's wheelbase and

they're worth the extra. If you get bored of the crush inside you can always sit on the roof for a while.

— Lonely Planet: Across Asia on the cheap (1973)

However, we are not on the main trail, and a bit of research hints at an option: a line from Rishikesh to the city of Pokhara in Nepal glances a small border crossing between Banbassa in India and Mahendranagar in Nepal. Ah-hah! Instead of following the Ganges, we could follow the spine of the Himalayas, squeeze through its foothills and the southern border of Nepal, through its wild west. Ten years ago, during the Nepalese civil war, travel advisories said to "exercise a high degree of caution" in the Mahakali and Seti regions. Well, that was ten years ago, right?

But all we can dig up is hearsay, old forum posts, confusing questions and conflicting recommendations. We distil information from the vapour of online rumour:

The border crossing is a bridge over the Mahakali river. It is highly unclear if foreigners can cross here. But rumours of visas sold for US dollars (bills in good condition please!) suggest that it is possible. But the visa is needed before crossing the bridge to the border. But the border guard is reported to be "many times drunk in the evening". But the bridge is only open between sunrise and sunset. But other times the bike path is open and the walkway is closed. But someone claims they hacked the border by chartering a bike taxi along the bike path, outside of opening hours. But no vehicles are permitted *unless* they are *not* passenger buses. The border police are "very friendly" unless they are "a bunch of thugs who harass travellers and extort their hard-earned money".

Just travelling the road up to the village Banbassa on the Indian side promises adventure. Trains go a long way around, but perhaps local buses can take us close, save us a day or two? We face a fistful of bad options, all dependent on transport modes that are advised to be "dangerous" because of "frequent accidents with multiple fatalities".

A tourist office provides a map with bus lines filled in in blue ballpoint pen. At Rishikesh's bus station, a very helpful man in a corrugated steel ticketing office suggests a route that might work: the bus line from Haridwar to Tanakpur passes through Banbassa just after midnight. He prints an itinerary and adds me on Facebook.

Well. Even if we make it to the border, and even if we make it across the border, we know nothing about what to do on the Nepalese side. One message board post outlines a taxi from the border to Mahendranagar, and a "terrible" bus to Pokhara.

One Dutch poster made up his mind just weeks before us: "I'm deliberately not going to make any Plan B, so that I focus all my strength...". That is his last post to the message board.

This is *our* Plan B: risking James' last days of travel on pushing through to Kathmandu airport, so he can fly home in time for school.

42

ASIDE: A NOTE ON CAULIFLOWER

Zigzag across the field outside the bed&breakfast on the Ganges valley's green wall. It must have rained. The tall grass is wet, the sky is overcast, the smell of earth is heavy. The path winds down through fields and between houses before nosediving through the ultra-commercial beehive of ashrams. I am joining the others for breakfast at their hotel but I am running late in the backstreets, alleys, cul-de-sacs and warning signs. In the village, the calm is replaced by clinking wind-chimes and the same om-shanti-shanti mantra CD that has been on repeat here since the mid-nineties. Cross the bouncy Laxman Jhula bridge with the river rushing underneath, hook a right, and there they are.

Order up tea, yoghurt with fruit and a slice of app... le... pie-ie-I-*I don't feel well*. I need to walk for a bit, get some air. Stand up, step into the street, head back to the bridge for some fresh Himalayan air.

Seconds later I grab my water bottle off the table, mutter "I'll be back" and head for the nearest sink instead. Bad stew yesterday?

You know how cauliflower look like little brains? Vomit so forcefully that little cloudy pieces of grey vegetables come out your nose. It really, *really* looks like you are literally puking your brains out.

43

TOMORROW THEN?

RISHIKESH, INDIA

Today my time at the top of the valley is up. Head down the fragrant meadow toward the Ganges again. Overcast and still. Silent. Down through the village again and across the suspension bridge to pick up James and start our race for the Nepalese border. Heavy rain clouds tumble down the green slopes on the opposite side. I swing into the hippies' hotel. Good morning to the café staff. Head down the stairs to the basement. Knock the door. No answer. No light under the door. Wait politely. Knock again. Still nothing. Kids these days! No padlock on the door, so they are in there. WAKEY WAKEY JAMIEBOY! BUS TIME!

The windowless cell smells like murder. Someone must have died in here; probably James. Fumble for the light switch. Yeah, the room certainly looks like a crime scene. There is a thin, tall body on the bed and it whines at the light and sound.

"Are you ill, man?" No reply. "Hey, are you alive?"

A miserable face emerges from under the pillow. He gestures to a saucepan balancing beside him on the bed. "There is a bowl of vomit here." There is. "Why is it green?"

We are not going to Nepal today, then. Being homeless now, I discreetly drop my backpack in James' dark plague cell and then enjoy apple pie and tea as the rain pours from the awning outside.

Once it stops: a day of strolling without a plan, walking around and around the river. Cross Laxman Jhula bridge, walk downstream, cross Ram Jhula bridge, walk upstream again, cross Laxman. Ask around for transport to the places between here and the border crossing at Banbassa. Bareilly, Haldwani, Tanakpur. Roorkee, Rampur, Haldwani.

Check in on the sick man in the basement.

"There's a bus to Tanakpur in an hour. Feeling better?"

"No," he whimpers from the dark.

I write home. Call Dad from a lopsided wooden balcony over the Ganges, wrapped up in a fleece against cold wind. The sun sets, and Eric and Cindii bring dense slices of black, moist "Best Chocolate Cake" from the German Bakery next door. In the evening, an intense thunderstorm totters on the valley walls; lightning passing from one side of the other.

I wait for the rain to let up a little, then hurry through wet and cold night down along the Ganges to an ashram where a restaurant is open late. Dark, spicy chai, and a raspy, interrupted Skype call home.

44

HOURS AND HOURS AND HOURS

RISHIKESH TO BANBASSA, INDIA

I ask James how he feels. He groans. We have lost two of the days we had to reach Kathmandu. I suggest coffee and some Best Chocolate Cake to get us on the road again. Another groan. "Too early to talk about cake, mate."

The day presents more rolling thunder in the distance, our teasers of Himalayan monsoon season. James gets back up of his bed, up from the basement and out into pale daylight. We make our way up to the bus stand to pick up tickets for the bus east to Banbassa. The face on the friendly man in the ticket shed lights up when we enter. "Yesterday bus! Big accident!" I do not ask for details I would prefer to not know about.

The hotel arranges a taxi from other side of Laxman Jhula. James and I say a final good-bye to our dreadlocked friends and jog through rain into a warm car that dashes down the narrow valley road, back to Haridwar. We drive past fields in rain and mist, little fires under corrugated steel awnings, and closer to town, market stalls. The silhouette of an impossibly tall Shiva statue looms in the drizzle.

The bus to Banbassa is parked in the terminal but doesn't leave for another two hours. We cosy up on its vinyl-clad benches to get out of the rain, and wait. I take my chances on a quick grocery run through the deluge to pick up drinks and snacks for the seven-hour ride. Closer to departure, salesmen stream through the bus with water, popcorn, cucumbers, blankets, tea, gold watches. We try to sleep. Headphones on, to close out the bustle of the station, lightning visible through closed eyelids, thunder felt through the bus's undercarriage. At dusk, we rattle off across a bridge and over dark Ganges, a field of rushing water glinting in twilight.

The road starts out bumpy. Surprisingly bumpy. It starts out bumpy and never, ever gets better. The bus vibrates. Shakes. Jolts. The entire carriage seems intent on destroying itself. The window pane tinkles in its fitting. We both have window seats, but there is no way to lean up against the window. Cranial bones would be fractured by the glass. Plating comes off the bus. Bags rain from the luggage shelves overhead. Poor James is still sick on the bench behind me.

We remember: "yesterday bus, big accident!" There are no seat belts, but there is a steel bar mounted in front of me – at teeth-level. Dear backpack on my lap, as a makeshift airbag. I hug it tightly.

Hours and hours and hours of shaking. Eyesight blurs. Can't feel my lower back. To stay somewhat put in my seat, I fold my legs against the seat in front but realise that cracked kneecaps do not heal well. During the night I entangle my arms in the bag's straps so we both stay put, and try to fall asleep. Two more hours of this.

I startle awake when James taps my shoulder. His tortured face is blurred by vibrations. He has bad news to share. It is just past midnight and we should be arriving in Banbassa soon, but his map app indicates that we are not even half-way. We are nowhere at best, on a mud track in Uttarakhand state, winding through what might have been villages but all we see is empty façades spilling garbage into night streets.

We stop at a night market for coffee and... skip food, for fear of being sick again. The firm ground feels spongy underfoot now that the world has stopped vibrating. After half an hour in the bitter Himalayan night, the bus honks its own special melody to call us back into its trembling frame. The black sky is clear and stars are white and impossibly many (though not as many as the bumps and potholes in the road, and their faint light is not as weak as the bus's suspension.)

At dawn, the world still rattles. Startle awake again. Still on the bus. Hours must have passed. Little houses on both sides of the road.

I check the time.

It has been *thirteen* hours.

James is not on the bus.

45

ON THE BRINK OF NEPAL, AND COLLAPSE

BANBASSA, INDIA TO MAHENDRANAGAR, NEPAL

The bus is rolling out of a town. Where am I, where is James, why is his bag still on the bench, where is the bus going, where will I be if I jump off and where will I end up if I stay on it? A scattershot of questions blurted out at the same time.

"Stop, stop. Please wait, stop. Banbassa?"

"This is Banbassa."

Where the hell is James? What do I do with his bag? Throw it off the bus? Leave it on? Still 100% groggy, I make a quick decision. Throw out my bag from the bus, scoop up James's bag to and a find couple of his notebooks on the floor. Stumble off onto dirt. My knees buckle. Every muscle hurts. I hope this was the right decision.

Down the road stands a tall, familiar silhouette, talking to a man about a horse. Why was James off the bus while his bag was on it? We never fully reconstruct how bus, bag, me, road, not on board, then horse, how it all happened, but we chalk it up to exhaustion and vibration madness.

As sick and tortured as we are, James is still capable of bartering for a room. We will not move a single step toward the border today. We collapse into cold beds in a bystander's family's home. Hours later, neither of us feel any better. We spend the day in bed entertained by South Park, stomach pains and hot showers poured from a red plastic bucket.

Where the hell is this place? Somewhere in the north-western corner of India, but during the night I have lost all sense of direction, distance or reality. There is a gap in my journey, a blank space that I can not mentally connect to yesterday. As in a dream, I walk around to buy water, Coke, chips to restore lost salts. The Hep A vaccination has not taken full effect yet, but I take my chances on very spicy noodles, fried in a wide pan over an open flame in the street, served in a flimsy plastic bag and eaten as finger food from the same bag. If this doesn't give me dysentery, nothing will.

Head back out again to look for an ATM *again*, but of course this is not a place to find the US dollars in good condition for the Nepalese visa. Do we have to figure out how go back (by terrible bus) for green paper money? The rumours on how to pay at the border are still unclear; maybe rupees are accepted. Maybe dollars are necessary. The hotel owner is not sure either, but we are not getting on a bus again. No sir. We take our rupee chances tomorrow.

We drift in and out of sleep. Read a little. Then rain hammers the roof again, and purple lightning blinks in the sky again.

Early, early in the morning, we charter a horse cart to take us to the border. It is about a kilometre down the road, past kids and grown-ups crossing on foot. The cart's wooden wheels crunch on sparse gravel. Bags loosely lashed to the planks, ourselves hanging on by hand. Through airy and green forest, spirits lifted by every clip-clop and by the walnut smell of horse. Still no clear indication if we can cross here, but even if we can we do not know how to get to Pokhara.

We hope to cross the Mahakali river on a rumoured bridge, continue through the town Bhimdatta on the far side, to the bus terminal in Mahendranagar. The horse service ends at a causeway leading out on the bridge. The bridge turns out to be the Sharda river barrage, all steel and concrete and machinery and dirt-pale water rushing under us into white spray clouds. The river irrigates a large area of Uttarakhand, while only a thin little canal leads off into Nepal; a fitting geopolitical illustration of the region. It is rumoured that a man-eating monster fish terrorises the riverbanks: cows and children lost to mutant catfish teeth.

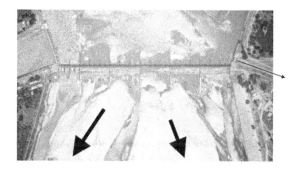

We sign out of India on the porch of a border villa, record our names in another large binder and chitchat with a stereotypical librarian who has ended up stuck at the very edge of India. We are still too weak to walk to the bus terminal by ourselves. We recruit a bicycle rickshaw, pedalled by a worryingly old man over difficult cobblestones. He drops us off at a Welcome to Nepal sign by a low, blue building, front façade open to the street. The immigration office is little more than a table on the lawn. It is a quick process. With visas paid for (in Indian rupees, no problem, Sir!), and affixed to our passports with glue stick, we can now walk the first few meters of the legendary final stretch of the Hippie Trail. Let's see if we can get down to Kathmandu. Half a country left to cross.

Next stop along that road: Mahendranagar, where we hope to find passage down to Pokhara. We choose between "Swastika Taxi" and another rickety local bus with paisley seats. Unfortunately, we took the bus again.

46

TRAGIC BUS

MAHENDRANAGAR TO POKHARA, NEPAL

A tiny clown bus, but that is fine. The worst bus ride in history is behind us. We can do this. Our bags are thrown up top as usual, and lashed down with bungee cord, where they can enjoy fresh air and ample space. We, on the other hand, sit folded up in our seats which would hardly fit a normal-sized dog, much less James and me. Our scalps brush against the paneling overhead, and knees shift around to find an angle where tired muscles do not cramp up.

When the bus rolls out on the road leading east from Mahendranagar, it shudders in a cacophony of bags bouncing, springs squeaking, windows rattling. It is 300 kilometres to Pokhara. Nervously: this bus is as bad as the one to Banbassa, nine more hours, haha! Ha ha ha. Damn.

The bench at the back of the bus is still free. There is headroom and leg space there. We untangle from the tiny seats by yanking our legs free, angling knees, and pulling ourselves out into the aisle by grabbing the luggage rack on the other side. The back of the bus will be our kingdom.

It is a terrible kingdom, though. It hangs far behind the rear axle, creating a lever mechanism that amplifies the vibrations of the bus.

> If you've ever ridden a see-saw for twelve hours you'll know the feeling. Make sure you get deluxe seats, they ... are within the bus wheelbase and they're worth the extra.
>
> — LONELY PLANET: ACROSS ASIA ON THE CHEAP (1973)

We are well "outside the wheel base," against the recommendations of the now 40-year old original Lonely Planet guide... A pothole bump to the rear wheels becomes a catapult shock to us in the back.

We cross a dry, stony riverbed. This bus hardly holds together on asphalt; driving it over football-sized boulders and caked mud is absurd. I am holding on to the seat in front with both hands, so I can do nothing when a shock sends my daypack into the air, back-flipping and crashing into the aisle, sliding out of sight.

A sequence of expressions during the first few hours: amused giggling, frustrated discomfort, and then glassy-eyed apathy. Boredom layers on top of torture. After four hours of simply holding on, the mind wanders. I have a book but focusing on a page in this long earthquake is impossible. I try to listen to an audiobook instead but there is no volume setting loud enough to drown out the squealing suspension and thundering bounces. I need to use one hand just to keep my headphones on my head. I try to record the unbelievable amplitude of the bus's swings and jolts on video, but it is – cross my heart and hope not to die on this bus – difficult to even aim the camera out the window.

At night, I try to lie down on the bench, arms and knees propped up against the seat in front, one hand holding on to a grey plastic handle, one hand gripping the bench seat just to keep myself in place. Windows half-open to the cold night in hope that fresh air will take the edge off the motion sickness. Wind tousles hair and dries eyes, but positioned like this, James has a much better chance of vomiting out of the bus instead of on the floor.

Looking up and out, the stars are grains of salt on ink. They swirl. I feel strange. Am I having a cosmic transcendental-astral projection experience, or is this a concussion?

This is how space shuttle re-entry looks on film. Shocks send me flying clean off the bench, high enough that I have time to clamp my teeth together before the hard landing. Once I miss the bench entirely on the way down.

I do not dare to lie on my back for fear of swallowing my tongue. Cramped grip on the bench cushion, cramped grip on my daypack, cramped grip with one boot wedged between the bench and the wall. Then the damn bench itself comes loose.

The run to Pokhara is like riding a bike down a staircase. Every few hours, the bus stops by the roadside. Pale but dogged Nepalese spill out of the bus for tactical vomiting. We weak and jelly-boned backpackers stumble out of the bus for fresh air and the full-body experience of a stable world in the dark. Then, back on the bus, like a roller coaster and we are going for another two hours.

The handle on the back of the seat in front of me is attached with just one screw, but it is the only fixed point in the entire world. A grey ear of rugged plastic that yanks at my arm and chafes my skin, but I feel I can trust it. I bounce like popcorn on the bench, holding on it with one hand. As long as I can keep my fist closed I will not fall out into the aisle. Fingers cramp up. After another few hours, the plastic handle bends, whitens and snaps off, and I must find something else to hold on to.

During one midnight halt, I look at the time. Realise something. We have had the same driver this entire time, and he has never left his seat. How he stays awake (and hopefully alert) is a mystery. I darkly hope that he is hopped up on high-grade amphetamines.

SEVERAL HOURS ARE LOST from memory, but the sky brightens. I can hardly see anything anymore. My eyeballs vibrate. But there are houses outside. Fields. And a bright-blue splotch high in the sky.

"Ja-a-A-M-mEs. I tHI-nk-k you'LL wAnt t-to sEe tHIs."

He clambers over to look out the window on my side. It is hard to see clearly – the window moves around a lot – but there they are. The first ones.

"BIG FUCKING MOUNTAINS!"

Here, at around 83°E, Himalaya spikes up. Outside the window, Dhaulagiri, Machhapuchhre and the Annapurnas parade the horizon.

47

DAYS ON THE LAKE
POKHARA, NEPAL

After five hours on the bus, I could not image how we would survive the rest of the trip. No specific idea of what would have killed us; I just had no idea how a human body could stay functioning through nine hours in a tumble dryer. When we arrive, it is morning again. That means the ride did not take nine hours, but *nineteen*.

I have no memory of arriving. I am in a cold room again. I have no idea where. I cannot remember how I got here. I am sore. I think I have frozen to this bed. Every part of me is a disembodied, remote ache. I remember a staircase. I think there were bathroom tiles somewhere. James got us off the bus, into a taxi, to a hotel, up some stairs and into beds.

The hotel advertises hot shower and wifi but the water is not heated "right now" and the wifi password is for the coffee shop across the street.

I change clothes. I find the broken-off grey plastic handle from the bus stuffed in my bag. I wonder why.

Between sleep and carbohydrates, life returns. The town treats us well, once we find better accommodation. A room with beds, a functioning hot shower. Pokhara sits on the shore of Phewa Tal (Lake Fewa), on the floor of crisscrossing valleys, a city of low houses with vibrant façades on either side of a boulevard where buffalo and mopeds dance around each other under heavy Banyan trees. Their trunks are painted pastel and, in their shade, beige little dogs monitor all passers-by. The boulevard is lined with restaurants and piles of North Fake trekking gear. When the sun sets, the street lights up with garish LED while the surface of Lake Fewa glows purple and red. Utility poles lean under the weight of crisscrossed wiring, thick bundles coming down the street and disappearing into Pokh@ra Cyber-Café. The city sprawls up and out into the valley corridors around, all crowned by the sharp, distant pyramid of an ozone-blue peak.

We dine on chicken in Nepalese spices and German bakery-style apple pie. The owner of the inn insists that we play chess on his porch while warm rain falls like a curtain in the garden.

On the northern shore of Lake Fewa, a sharp peak rises to a lookout platform with clear views of the Annapurna mountain range. James vanishes up the narrow trail and its winding stone staircases; I follow, weak and slow. The heat is punishing, but the air clears once we climb out of the jungle. Below us: Pokhara and the lake. Above us: wild hawks and paragliders on warm updrafts from the valley. Further up: vivid houses in Sarangkot village, children and goats and narrow alleys winding up the hill. Two or three hours later, the stairs pass through a smattering of hilltop hotels, cross a road and then take off sharply upward again. They lead through market stalls filled with scarfs and trinkets, through a gate and a little temple, to a platform, a ladder and a ledge, and then there is nothing between us and Annapurna II, III and IV, and the sharp ax-head of Machhapuchhre, the Fishtail.

POKHARA IS the starting point for the Annapurna Circuit, one of the most legendary treks of Nepal, if not the world. It leads up the Marsyangdi valley a half day's drive east of Pokhara. The trek follows the Marsyangdi river in behind the Annapurna peaks. A week's walk into the valley, the trek turns north and rises steeply to cross the Thorong La pass at 5416 meters. On the far side of the pass lies the forbidden kingdom of Mustang, the capital Lo

Mantang and the sacred city of Muktinath. What mystical names! The Annapurna Circuit pours back down south along the Kali Gandaki river for another week, back to Pokhara. Expect 2-3 weeks. A kind lady at a trekking centre outside our hotel arranges a trekking permit and wishes me good luck.

James and I rent a little boat and go rowing on Lake Fewa at dusk. Rolling mountains recede into those familiar shades of lavender. Out here, the air is cool and free of scents. The prism ridge of Annapurna II hangs in the evening sky, high above Sarangkot on the northern shore. After the storm of impressions in India, Nepal offers clarity. One colour at a time (pale purple), one sound at a time (oar splashing) and one place at a time (this lake).

After sunset, cool winds rush out of the Pokhara valley, rustling the bunting prayer flags strung across the boulevard. The word "trek" is everywhere: on advertisements, on equipment shops, on restaurants, on hotels, on signs, on jackets and on cars. Every side street begins with a tall pole filled with hotel signs: ten or thirty enamelled plates advertising the Pokhara Peace Home, Century Guest House, Teacher Krishna Lodge or the Hotels Star Light, Annapurna Lake View, Travel Inn, Lake Diamond, Peace Ganga, Serenity, Avocado, and Celesty Inn, which is where we sleep like puppies under the care of a radiant, smiling chess-player in a crisp suit.

I still have time for one more adventure, but James' days on the road are running out. But we did make it all the way across the border, through Nepal, all the way to these Big Fucking Mountains.

We briefly consider renting a car and just driving on to Kathmandu, a day's drive east into the country. From there, I could trek into the Khumbu region instead and up to the base camp of Mount Everest, Sagarmāthā. I could see the roof of the world in time for my birthday. The allure of a final, last-minute change of plans.

But one evening, we take a parting dinner at the Olive Café; play a final game of magnetic travel chess over dessert. The restaurant lights a fire. Sharp aroma of juniper twigs and tourist brochures burn with green flames. At dawn James vanishes east to go home to Australia, and I go north into the Marsyangdi valley, and into Annapurna.

PART V

ANNAPURNA

I leave Pokhara in the morning. A cold rain drums the roof of the taxi; the hotel owner waves to me from the porch. It is recommended to leave early, to arrive in Besi Sahar mid-day, and to reach the village of Ngadi Bazaar before dark.

A breakfast of tea and eggs. The air is thick with anticipation from an unusual density of trekkers who pace the gravel between rows of buses painted with ornaments, eyes and names. Above of buses, the Annapurna massif hangs from the morning sky.

48

TROPICAL ASCENT

POKHARA TO CHAME, NEPAL

On the bus to Besi Sahar, trekkers pick each other out from the crowd and clump up. I share a section of the bus with a German engineer on his way back from a posting in Beijing, and an Italian vagabond on his way generally east for the moment. The road climbs narrow valleys into the Lamjung district. A child throws up beside me but I can only briefly look away from the edge of the road which falls steeply away. Everywhere is deep-chlorophyll forest ochre dust and grey cinder-block houses.

The three of us, Germany, Italy and I, arrive in Besi Sahar around mid-day. After a second breakfast on plastic chairs in the dusty street, there are no more excuses not to get on the trail, so…

what happens now? I expected there to be a banner or a ticket booth or something, but we just need to walk from here... for about three weeks. An unceremonious departure out of town, over a bridge and there is the Marsyangdi valley leading up into the Annapurnas.

The magic of the Himalayas does not begin at the suburbs of a small country town. Only gravel roads and school children on their way home for the day. In sections, the road widens to allow jeeps that zip between villages, trailing choking dust-clouds behind them. Then, the path leads onto ancient stone stair steps and soon we zigzag the Marsyangdi river over narrow suspension bridges that bounce when walked on. When the sun begins to set and the landscape reddens in front of us, we reach Ngadi Bazaar. The gravel road winds through houses and yards on both sides, and we decide to call it a day: our Day One. We rent beds in a teahouse built around a rose garden and eat dinner by a brook. The valley goes dark, but at the far end, mount Manaslu's peak burns red in the sunset.

The way up to Bahundanda village is a knee-killing staircase skirting along the edges of terrace plantations of rice and lentils, where sunlight filters into the valley like curtains. Birds turn up their volume where the road curves left onto sunlit stretches and fall silent again after rightward curves back into cold shade.

The valley widens, roughens. High up on the sides, backhoes and other construction equipment claw at the hills. The road disappears into a gravel pit under a thick dust cloud where more yellow bulldozers and diggers sit. A hydroelectric plant is being built here under a Chinese contract. Signs in Chinese line corrugated steel barracks where we try to find a way around and/or through.

To the Annapurna trekking region, construction is a dilemma. Old-school trekkers who came through in the decades after the trail opened in 1977 still tell misty-eyed stories about the real Nepal, about how the only roads were goat-paths winding through rural villages (and their poverty). But the Lamjung district is authentic in the sense that people actually live here, and need roads, communications, internet and healthcare as much as anyone else. This is not a park or a reserve. The real Nepal has free wifi. It changes, so the trail passes a construction pit this year. Little bunting flags wrapped around barbed wire mark the trail on a dull, sandy slope around a deep gouge in the ground and back down on the far side.

Bahundanda sits on a green mountain pass above rice terraces, and the final stretch feels vertical as the morning air starts to boil. We crest the pass, drain all water bottles in the damp heat, and refill. Repeat. A few biscuits to replace lost salt. Leaned on our backpacks in the sun, we observe two figures drag themselves the last few hundred stair-steps up to the village. A young Danish man on an unplanned round-the-world walkabout that has taken him from New York to the Himalayas, and a Hungarian bartender looking for a trekking challenge. Our little crew is expanded to five and we drop their names too, in favour of their nationalities. Sweden, Germany, Italy, Denmark and Hungary leave Bahundanda as Team Europa.

On the far side of Bahundanda, the path leads down again through a grove of knotty, bent trees. It cuts in between dusty walls and under the shade of the trees, a leafy tunnel. Right around a bend, the jungle clears up and the valley floor drops away into a kilometre-wide basin. A long sight-line up the valley shows us just how far away the Annapurna range is, and how the only way there is to keep walking thin path lines along sweeping lines of terraced plantations, long enough that their ends are out of sight, and large enough that their scale is difficult to reckon. The valley is a large optical illusion that swells and shrinks.

We take lunch in Ghermu, at a teahouse perched right on a

high ridge above the river, delineated by wild bamboo and little forest fires signalled by grey smoke plumes. We end up sharing tables with two trekkers from Wales and Canada. Canada lives a dream: he works six months of the year as a wilderness firefighter at the very edge of British Columbia, and then travels for six months – like my cave-mate in Turkey. Now that is an alternative career to consider.

Next, a punishing, hour-long switchback gravel climb up to Jagat village. It is not the stretch marked "steep hot climb" on the map, however. We will get to that tomorrow. Jagat sits in a narrow ravine beneath grey-black blocks of Himalayan stone. We are invited to dine in the courtyard of a tall, tower-like house; hard beds at the top of stairs and ladders; thin plywood walls and plastic windows. On a wall is a badly photoshopped poster of the "Paris Tower"; a monstrous Eiffel tower looming over what looks like Rome against the backdrop of Mount Fuji.

We fight the incline, eyes on the ground, all I see is gravel. Gravel roads, gravel landslides, gravel crunching underfoot, and the dry riverbed at Tal. The road is gouged out from the cliff side, a half-tunnel with no wall on the right side, trafficked by donkey trains, cling-clanging cowbells. Then into scraggly trees and dark rock. Then along a path so narrow that I have to mind not scraping my backpack on the wall, mind not tumbling down to the bottom. Then past a humming beehive the size of my leg, smeared on the cliffside.

A string of electricity poles snakes along the path, then up high on the valley walls, then back down across the river, through villages. The road also winds in and out of side-valleys. Up ahead, a rock face several hundred meters high, with a thin, wavy arc drawn across it from left to right – that is the road.

Team Europa thins out: Germany with walking poles races ahead; overloaded Sweden at the rear. Once the path starts to make its hair-raising way up the cliff face, the scale of the valley becomes clear. It reaches up far above the road, and it falls all the way down there, with us at its majestic middle. At the road's apex, there is a roadside shrine to memorialise workers lost to its construction.

In Dharapani, we settle in for a long and uneventful evening and night, gathered around a fire in the tea-house, jackets on and all, and just wait for dinner. Brief showers of ice-cold rain as the sky darkens into a milky blue.

Prayer flags flutter restlessly in the garden, as if something is happening just around the bend, the bend where my road on the Hippie Trail turns due west for the first time and leads away from Kathmandu for a couple of weeks.

I recall the entire road here: replay all the long days on trains through Europe and through India, comfortable nights on Iranian buses and traumatic nights on Himalayan buses. A million steps taken on sidewalks, train platforms, deserts, alleys. A slow approach on my own schedule and the disjointing night-flight over Pakistan.

Plenty of time out in the open world, feeling connected and free and woven into the tapestry of humanity.

Now these mountain walls rise to cut off the outside world, both in terms of topography and in terms of radio signal. They promise that the coming weeks will be an expedition into my own head.

After Thoche, we keep climbing through a slanted, hot jungle, dragging ourselves up by tree roots and high steps. I promise myself not to stop unless I 1) vomit, 2) faint, or 3) miss a step.

Just before Timang, I reach a group of people lined up with their cameras pointed into the open air behind me. I turn around.

We have ascended out of the tropic forest, and behind us the horizon is the entire eastern end of the massif. From the rooftop of a hot pink teahouse, the view of mountains, peaks, ice fields is unobstructed; absolutely clear.

In Chame, we celebrate. It is Italy's birthday and we party hard: lentils and rice, half a beer each, and then fall sleep at nine o'clock.

49

LAND OF THE ANCESTORS

CHAME TO GHYARU, NEPAL

This is where we go when we die, a local explains, pointing to a smooth, snow-covered slope up the other side of the valley. He is Gurung, one of Nepal's ethnic groups, a people living in the valleys of central Nepal. They have run the trans-Himalayan salt trade route to Tibet since forever.

The *Oblē* dome, the after-life mountain, the mountain of heaven, is a gigantic, smoothly curved sheet of rock tilted up like a chip of paint from the valley bed. In the Gurung proto-Buddhist tradition, the Land of Ancestors is on the far side of the Oblē. If you shout the name of a deceased ancestor up the mountain, you can hear them shout their name back down.

> A direct course was chosen, if possible with small loss of incline. Steep inclines were accepted only as an exception.
>
> — Important Trade Routes in Nepal and Their Importance to the Settlement Process, Graafen (1993)

That paper lies. "Nepali flat" means "less than a hundred meters up or down". The trek itinerary summarises one of today's merciless hiking stretches: *Distance: 1.5km. Duration: 90 minutes.* The forest switches from leafy jungle to sparse pines and we keep shrinking under the peaks around us. Splish-splash through waterfalls and climb up switchbacks, passing mule trains saddled with bags of rice.

Heavy bursts of icy rain follow us through the forests, so we stop at a tea lodge to pull rain covers over the bags. Stock up on a few extra emergency Snickers. The rain brings out a heavy scent of pine trees that fills the basins and blows away on the crests.

When the Gurung die, their spirits come up here. The living shepherd the spirits up the mountain and force them to cross over to their ancestors because a spirit is often unwilling to go. It might not have understood that it is dead yet. It is led to a pool of water and lies down to drink from it. This is "forget-water," so the spirit can forget life.

The spirit is sternly told to stay in the Land of Ancestors and not come back – it is not welcome around the houses anymore. But be patient, spirit: the rest of your family will join you – eventually. Once in the Land of Ancestors, the spirit can choose to be reborn, but Gurung tradition, there is no karmic evaluation before rebirth. So, spirit: if you decide to return, the priests recommend being reborn as someone important or skilful.

We walk into the first snow. Just before Pisang, we drag ourselves up over the 3000-meter mark and breaths become shorter. We huddle around the wood stove in a charming, pink-and-purple lined teahouse, and we watch Into Thin Air on a bootleg DVD in the dining hall while a heavy dinner is cooking in the kitchen. Rain on the windowpanes, but we have an unobstructed view all the way back to the moonlit Oblē dome.

Pisang has a post office on the hayloft of a barn. Together with Canada, Jr., the latest addition to Team (ahem) Europe, I climb a dark wooden stair to a low-ceilinged office and hand over a thick stack of postcards filled with complaints about altitude, oxygen and gravel inclines, to be postmarked in the high Himalayas.

The peaks around the valley have grown tall enough to cut into the overcast sky, and disappear into white. The trail snakes along their walls, westward toward the district capital of Manang and after that, the Thorong La pass.

I think about those postcards, on their way out of here, sent from between two rows of Himalayan teeth. I feel delightfully alone, as if I am *behind* the world somehow. On the trails between delicious village names – Ngadi, Syange, Dharapani, Timang, Thanchowk, Bhratang – this solitude becomes more than a situation; more than a state. Solitude grows into a concrete thing, a precious object that I can cultivate and grow.

I let myself slip behind the rest of the group. Being off-season, it is only a matter of a few minutes until I have this mountain cathedral all to myself. Just being up here is like stealing a few weeks from the world. But when the others have disappeared around a corner and I am completely alone, something else comes over me. A sweet sensation flickering between mindful presence and a weird sense of detachment.

But I could be alone at home as well. This is something else. The moment blends with remoteness, with being unreachable. Not by distance – a resort beach in Thailand is much further from home – but remote by obscurity. I return to those postcards in the saddlebag of a donkey train going across suspension bridges and down stone stairs to Besi Sahar, imagine how they are trucked to Pokhara, maybe put on a domestic postal flight to some mail station in Nepal's capital – but even then, they are still in mythical Kathmandu. Me, myself, I am going the other way, further up into the mountains. This is time for me. I knew I would love being alone. But why was loneliness in the hotel room back in Amritsar so very difficult, then?

WE WALK for a stretch with two doctors, enterprising women from New Zealand and the Ukraine, on their way up to Manang to open the seasonal clinic in Manang, where they will provide altitude consultations to trekkers and volunteer healthcare for the locals. How many discreet questions about altitude sickness can I fit into normal conversation? We are firmly above 3000 meters now, which is at the beginning of the altitude sickness zone. Walking even slightly uphill requires frequent stops to keep breathing normally.

Somewhere up ahead is that part of the map marked "steep climb".

We may have lost the trail again. We are supposed to follow it up a steep incline, but it runs slightly downhill instead. I look at the line of electric poles that runs along the track to see if they lead towards a teahouse somewhere. The line turns sharply off to the right, up the side of the valley. And sure: a switchback staircase and colourful backpacks zigzagging up to the *chhorten* pillar visible on the map. Δ altitude: +400 meters. *Hell* no.

But hell yes, of course. Half-way up, a donkey skull hangs from a branch, turning in the wind. I rest on a makeshift bench of layered stones, feet planted to not slip back on the gravel. The two doctors pass by on their way to Manang, soaring up the hill. I tilt my head far back to see up the path where red, blue, yellow backpacks work their way up. At least twenty switchbacks left.

I claw myself over the crest, to where everything is grey and white stone around the burning golden top of the chhorten pillar. Ghyaru teahouse sits on a south-facing balcony, and once I turn around, there she is: Annapurna II, prism ridge barely visible against the white sky. How wonderful to look at her from the north when just a week ago I was in Pokhara, admiring her from the south.

But! Something is missing! My sleeping bag is gone! Damn. It must have fallen off on the way up here. No no no. Not that climb again. Not down *and* up. But I must. I wave to Germany: I am going back down to look for it.

Then I look down the valley again. A soft cylinder rolls and bounces as if it were made for it. Best case, my sleeping bag is stuck in a tree somewhere on the slope, but most probably it is bobbing merrily down the Marsyangdi river, on its way back to Besi Sahar.

Hell no. I will rent blankets for the next two weeks.

Toodeloo bye-bye, sleeping bag.

Time for tea.

50

LOST, AND FOUND

GHYARU TO MANANG, NEPAL

Manang, the main town on the trail, is within a day's reach and reason enough to take longer steps. Hot showers? Better food? Better beds? Comfort? We look forward to a couple of rest days, altitude acclimatisation and hopefully better information about weather and snow depth up ahead. After we leave Manang we will remain above 4000 meters, and then up above 5000 meters, until we go over the Thorong La pass.

In the afternoon, I am slow out of Nyagdi, and end up behind Team Europa. The trail over the Ghyaru and Nyagdi villages has peaked, overlooking the Annapurna peaks before crashing down to the bottom of the valley again, where Manang lies. As soon as the others are out of sight again, I can overlook an incredible scenery that is all mine.

The moment fades as the trail comes up to a steep slope down through a pine forest, where a Californian couple have paused to look for a safe/sane way down. The slope is ice and mud, thawing and melting. The trail itself disappears into the dirt. There is no slow way down.

Slaloming between trees, I crash down into the bottom of the basin. Cannot see the Californians up through the trees anymore. I push on out of the forest to try to find the trail again, because the circuit probably does not run through these thorny bushes. I see the first buildings of Brakha ahead, and aim for their rooftops. I will be back on the trail in a few minutes.

But coming closer to them, they turn out to be abandoned shepherd huts. This is not the circuit at all. Not good. I really am off the trail, alone. The basin slopes up sharply on three sides. Did I come down into the wrong valley? I am too exhausted to go back up to Nyagdi and try again. It is silent here, except the distant whistle of jet winds over the peaks on the south side.

The sun sets rapidly, visibly. The gap between the sun and the Gangapurna ridge meters out the time to sunset, to dusk and then dark. Hard to tell when the sun will dip behind the mountains, because the peaks are covered in clouds. I might have an hour before the shadows come rushing down the south wall of the valley, or much less.

The afternoon sun is blazing down here, but the night will be cold. The map is useless: the basin could be *this* green area with curvy lines around it, or *that* green area with curvy lines around it. I really, really hope I am not separated from Manang by an hour-long climb, or worse.

Stop, Think, Orient, Plan. I just have to follow the Marsyangdi khola westward to Manang. As long as I can make my way down to the main valley again, there are only two ways out of here: right, and wrong. I fish out my Christmas present, the compass, and take out the direction south, deeper down toward the river and hope I am not too late to reach town before dark. Get stuck in ankle deep mud traversing a field. The Annapurna Circuit trail must cut across this basin *somewhere*. If I gamble time and cross the basin, I should come across the trail. But I can't find it. I might be too high up on the opposite side already. The wind is picking up, and bad clouds pour over the Gangapurna ridge.

Wait – ankle deep mud? Why is there mud here when the rest of the ground is dry?

The soil is soaked by a little concrete block that leaks water. There are water taps on the trail that look just like this. And yes! Red-white trail marks on its front. RECORD LEVELS OF RELIEF! Just seconds later: Hey! The Californians! Wait! Celebratory Snickers for everyone! Hooray for life!

We march together on a wide gravel road along a rock desert. Passing Brakha with its famous monastery, it is tempting to stop for the night, but the others have surely reached Manang by now. It is just another couple of kilometres along the road, last evening sun red on the rocks. Once through the mani gate outside Manang, the wind picks up in my back and pushes me up the ramp to the city.

Town.

Eh, village.

ONE MIGHT EXPECT restlessness after a week of walking, with 80 kilometres stomped into the ground and 2700 meters ascended, and then just stopping. But no, it is a blessed thing to wake up and not go anywhere. Or to walk up the main street and then turn around and go back. To sit down in the sun without any intention of getting back up and out. To order another serving of crispy apple pie, please, and take an hour to eat it. And another cup of tea, please.

The idea, the point, the lesson of the Annapurna Circuit is taking shape. Being briefly lost in the Himalayas yesterday seems trivial today. The path here is linear, and not only in the sense that we are on a narrow trail through straight valleys – it is also linear in the sense that there are no options. Forward, or not forward.

Things to do: walk, eat, sleep, repeat. One activity: to do the right thing. The only way out: do the right thing. Put one foot in front of the other enough times to get to the end. There are no other duties. Nothing to prioritise. Nothing to choose from. The circuit is difficult but I know I will finish, because giving up now would *also* require walking for a week. It is rare to have the simple thing also be the right thing. Oh, I wish, I wish, I wish to hold on to this clarity when I return home. The clarity of having one thing to do, of having no distractions, and of making surrender difficult.

~

MANANG IS a Wild West town of a few thousand inhabitants, built on the sides of a single stone road running a few hundred meters from one end to the other. We shack up in cold little bungalows behind a large inn. Four timbered floors around a narrow courtyard, with boots, bags, crampons, hiking poles, jackets, scarves, goggles, backpacks and blankets piled up around all the wooden pillars.

The group's Welshman fits right into the environment, fits into the Wild West fantasy of being on the run through remote villages. Mr. Wales' travels are financed by his previous employer. After leaving the company, he accidentally remained on the payroll and his salary kept paying out. They will surely notice one day and possibly come after him, but hopefully he is far away by then.

Warm lamp-light filters down through cross-hatched shadows and pours out of the dining hall. Long dinners of another round of pasta, yak burger, garlic, Tibetan bread with honey, apple pie; all huddled around an oil drum stove pumping out heat, melting all stiffness out of muscles. The doctors sit down at our table after a day of getting the clinic in order. High season will begin in a few weeks and their altitude sickness lectures will be packed. We get the gist over dinner, with laminated handouts.

The Annapurna and Gangapurna alpine walls shine electric white, and we take short acclimatisation walks up their slopes before coming down again, short of breath and tan and rosy-cheeked.

In the evenings, we visit a Manang cinema: all bundled up in down jackets and boots, on fold-up garden chairs in a basement presenting bootleg copies of *Seven Years in Tibet* and *Into the Wild* from a laptop and projector. We buy popcorn. A heater blows warm air at our feet. A cat sneaks in, walks unhurriedly across legs and laps before bunching up on me for warmth.

It is hard to sleep at night. It is cold, and the thin air makes the body wake up, restless, already short of breath, and filled with doubt. Clarity: gone. The road ahead is still so terribly long. Not only long measured by distance, but also by days. Time never runs slower than during insomnia or when short of breath. If the hours until dawn feel like weeks, what will the next week feel like? Perhaps I can not do this. But there is no other way out of here. In this night, clarity feels like helplessness.

I sneak out into the night to breathe deeper. The night is ink and filled with stars above the shimmering white wedge of the Gangapurna icefall.

51

ASIDE: MECHANIZED PRAYER

Everywhere we go, there is a chant from weak laptop speakers, playing an mp3 on repeat or a long Youtube track repeatedly restarted by the teahouse owner. It is the same recording everywhere: *Om mani padme hum*, perpetually. The same mantra is painted on the stones of *mani* walls, printed on bunting flags and embossed on prayer wheels. One of the oldest and largest such prayer wheels in the region is in the *gompa*, a monastery, in Brakha, which we passed on the way Manang. The words "nice gompa →" are spray-painted on a water spout, showing the way.

The gompa is closed most of the day, but the guidebook says you can ask around in the village for a key. A couple of Germans over there already have it, so we join them up the stairs to the monastery.

The tall door to the gompa creaks inward into darkness. A narrow hallway leads directly left, past dusty paintings of the gompa and oversized monks that work on the roof, pray outside and one monk is chased by a dog. Behind a heavy curtain, the prayer wheel stands on its axle, as big as a car. Out around the trail, mani wheels are made from tin cans rattling on their axes, swept into clattering rotation by passing hands. The huge mani wheel in Brakha needs full body effort and a good grip on the smooth metal letters to turn. It booms and clangs in the somber corridor.

It is filled with mantras written on paper slips, and om mani padre hum is hammered into the bronzed metal itself. Mantras are series of syllables that echo, or reflect, "basic sounds" of the universe; sounds that invoke aspects of cosmos. The om mani padme hum mantra has six syllables, each resonating as generosity, perseverance or patience. By reciting it or reading it, its effects go into the world, but it is just as effective to spin a mani wheel, a sort of prayer mill, with the mantra written on it or in it – as long as it is done with intention. There are little pendants and hand-held wheels with the mantra printed onto microfilm for extra efficacy. And instead of mantras written on paper slips stored in a hand-turned wheel, why not mantras written in text files stored in a stack of spinning DVDs? The online retailer "TibetTech" offers 1.3 trillion copies of the mantra in their most expensive DVD mani wheel.

52

CROSSING THORONG LA

MANANG TO MUKTINATH, NEPAL

Out of Manang onto a snowy two-day ascent toward Thorong La pass, the highest trekkable mountain pass in the world (5414masl). Trekkers frequently have to turn back due to weather or altitude sickness. We hear about failed attempts, renting donkeys, flying across by helicopter or just giving up, going back down east again.

There are two plans for crossing the pass. Both strategies need to clear the pass's highest point before 10AM and descend the far side before the sun-warmed air stir up difficult winds that whistle through the pass between the Thorong and Yakwakang peaks.

A. Stay at Thorong Pedi camp at the foot of the pass, acclimatise overnight at 4450m, and do a long day trip over the entire pass, down to Muktinath on the far side. To cross the pass before 10AM, this strategy requires getting up at 3-4AM.

B. Pass Thorong Pedi, skip the acclimatisation and attempt to sleep at altitude in Thorong High Camp at 4880m, to shorten the trek by a few hours. From High Camp, the pass can be crossed by sleeping in until 5AM or so.

We have chosen plan B: go directly to high camp and sleep at altitude, as Team Europa is still in good shape and unanimously prefers a shorter morning ascent. Two days in Manang prepared us well: investigating whether to buy crampons or to trust our shoes, asking for weather and snow coverage reports, doing laundry, resting up. We have what we need – everyone except careless Denmark, who believes he can cross the pass with his feet in plastic bags tucked into worn-out Nikes that he has walked around the world from Copenhagen. Will your feet freeze or will they rot, *mand?*

Black-grey-white pyramids rise ever steeper around us. It is as if we are not gaining altitude but sinking deeper and deeper below their bases. There is a lonely two-story teahouse at a bend in the road, built on a dry, cold valley side, ochre and dark yellow against bright peaks that sting our eyes. We settle in in early afternoon, rest and acclimatise to the altitude. A group of Israeli post-military-service backpackers share the dining hall under a plastic roof. We wait for evening and play cards around the wood stove when one of their guides excitedly wave for us to come outside in the cold. He is shouting something in Nepali, but he is insistent – no! He is shouting "snow leopard!" Come! Come!

Against the rocky slope on the far side of the valley, something moves. A spot. But the valley is dusky and far and grey and the air is thick with breath hanging in the cold air, and maybe we are just kidding ourselves. But maybe it was a snow leopard.

In an hour a full moon lights up the titanic triangles around us. We are in the middle of it now.

~

CAN'T SLEEP. Still wake up several times every night, short of breath and with racing pulse, frustration, panic. Turning over in bed is exhausting. I don't know what to do when lying down in a bed is not enough to catch my breath. Dawn comes again. Not sure I have slept yet, but we leave earlier than usual too. A relatively short walk up to High Camp, but every step is shortened accordingly.

In the shaded parts of the valley, frozen puddles shatter underfoot. In the sunny parts, gloves come off, sunglasses come down from foreheads and sleeves are rolled up in baking heat. Marsyangdi Khola, the river we have followed since Besi Sahar ten days ago, disappears out of sight behind valley walls. We cross long inclines lengthwise, across treacherous patches of gravel marked LANDSLIDE AREA (correct!) on tilting signs. Stones tumble and skip down from the steep mountainsides on our left; the river sputters and bubbles far below on our right. Our group thins out as everyone finds their own pace on the narrow path. Diamox, the altitude sickness prophylactic, makes my fingers tingle so bad I grit my teeth just tightening backpack straps. We turn a valley corner every twenty minutes, hoping to see the village of Thorong Pedi somewhere up ahead.

Thorong Pedi is three or four low buildings and a sign to Thorong La pass that points straight up the rocky side of the mountain. It is not a village, but a station. It is clearly more modern than anything else on the trail – there is a proper reception desk, sliding glass doors, freshly printed posters on walls – but there is no water tap here. There is only bottled water, and each bottle costs as much as a full dinner in the plains below. There is a simple explanation for this modernity at the end of the valley, the few houses and the lack of water: all of Thorong Pedi burned down recently.

The path disappears up the side of the Thorong mountain into a tilted rock desert that must be zigzagged up. Oh hell. We might as well get it done with; shrug on backpacks again and lean into the mountainside. 30° incline, this time into snow and rock. We walk in bursts of a few minutes, then rest a few minutes. Ten meters here, twenty meters there. I could throw a rock between each place we rest in. Smile at an alpine helicopter pad, no more than an H stomped into the snow. Wherever there is a rock to sit down on, I collapse and wait, breathing heavily, almost leaning against the steep slope. I have a dry cough.

This murderous incline to High Camp makes up almost ten percent of the total altitude gain since Pokhara. It is hard work, but we have Chulu's and Genjang's peaks around us. Birds drift by far below in the valley, and below the birds are the matchbox-sized buildings of Thorong Pedi.

The final hundred meters take ten minutes to cover in deep, melting snow slush. But here it is. High Camp. Low-slung, long stone buildings among rock and snow, like a moon base. After a hearty meal, we trudge even higher to a stone cairn on a small peak above the camp, with a view of the trail over the pass. It looks fucking dangerous.

High Camp quickly falls into lavender night-shade between the peaks. Headlamps sail around in the dark between the buildings. There is anticipation in the air. Tomorrow, we will see if we can get over to the other side, we will know whether we should have opted for crampons and we will feel what another 600 meters of altitude does to us. A few tiny snowflakes fall through the beams of light, threatening a difficult crossing if it turns into real snowfall. Bedtime is around 8PM. The air in the dorm rooms is just as cold as outside in the courtyard. We rent extra blankets and bottles of warm water and go to bed fully dressed. Before dawn, before Thorong La heats up in the morning sun, before mid-day winds flare up, we will wolf down breakfasts of porridge, eggs, coffee, Tibetan bread, hot water, and then walk out into the dark.

I cannot sleep. Diamox causes frequent outhouse visits, out into the black-blue night. It is so, so cold, but not much of a change from my bed – the door to our cabin does not shut properly. Snow whirls in. Signore Italy has already fallen asleep on the other side of the room. If he had not, I would have asked him: if we make it across the pass tomorrow, how far, how much longer could we go? How many weeks could I keep doing exactly this? Just lace up my boots every morning and walk until bedtime? Is the limit a distance in kilometres, or a duration in weeks? How long could I stay here behind the mountains? Could I walk all the way to Kathmandu? To the airport? Just set a goal, one foot in front of the other, positive thinking, perseverance.

The difficult question: if we can't make it over tomorrow, and not in the next few days – how long do we wait? When do we admit defeat? And how long will the way back feel, backtracking a trail of disappointment?

Please, body, just go to sleep. I will need this rest tomorrow. One foot in front of the other.

At around 4AM, a group of twenty in total gruntingly take the pre-ordered breakfast and drink a couple of mugs of hot water before lining up outside in the dark, headlamps lancing into the night. Pick our way along a narrow ice trail. I am one of the last in line, in my own puddle of blue light. Carefully ascend an ice staircase, with one hand on the mountain on the left. To the right: empty space. I am relieved I can not really see the bottom of the frozen slope that opens up no more than a meter to my right, leading down to who-knows-where.

The trail of headlamps, like a glowworm zigzagging up an unseen landscape – how the hell? where are they going? how did they get up that high? is there even a path that way? are they flying? Then they wink out, one by one, as they crest an unseen ridge, and I have fallen far behind. I slip a little on the ice steps, try to claw my toes into it through rubber soles, *do not move a muscle*–

We cross a bridge where the far end has snowed in completely, and we must climb off sideways at the bridgehead. Follow footprints over ice and gravel, into a vast, moonlit ice-field. Behind us, the horizon turns deep blue. Ahead of us, to either side, two gatepost mountain peaks. As sunrise hits their summits, they light up orange, more than 700 meters above us.

My water bottles have frozen, two ice pendulums hanging off my shoulder straps. We make a quick stop for tea in a shelter, piled in on long benches against the walls, stumbling around with frozen backpacks and stiff shoes, grinning and thawing.

We pass the 5300-meter mark. Inhaling deeply and slowly does nothing to help the lactic acid burn; nothing to help the shortness of breath but the sun is up now, warming the air. Because there is almost five kilometres less atmosphere between us and the sun, my skin burns under ultraviolet. SPF 50 does little at this altitude. The backs of my hands tan to a shade of purple, dry and scaly. But it is alright. We are on the moon. The edges of the pass bend upwards to both sides. We turn around and look the Chulu peaks straight in the eye. An illusion, of course: those peaks are more than another thousand meters higher than we are.

The trek never ends, just more and more white sloping upwards. No sense of progress. No air. Still moving slowly, slowly. Frequent stops. We clump together in smaller groups. Some fall behind while others are still capable of racing ahead. We wait. We go back. Make sure everyone is still with us.

We reach the stupa at Thorong La pass just after eight in the morning, at 5414m and at just about half of normal air pressure. Unload backpack, lie down in the snow, stretch, try to thaw out camera batteries in my armpit.

The descent on the backside of Thorong La turns out to be worse. At this time of year, the pass freezes every night but thaws out every morning. It is a steep, frustrating descent on mushy, difficult ground, shedding 1700 meters of altitude in just a few hours. A slow crash down through slush, mud, stone, snow. Eardrums pop.

We long to reach level ground on the Mustang plateau far below, but the altitude does not give in. It is like diving with a life-vest.

Long slogs through mudslides; slippery descents on slopes that would be hairy to even ski down. Thorong La eats my ankles, my knees, thighs, lower back, both my trekking poles, shoes and all my hope. Thorong La does not to let go. As a final insult after hours' descent on swollen knees, it leads me out on a muddy outcropping and ends in sharp drop into a labyrinth of thorny bushes. I can *see* the next teahouse where the strongest members of our expedition are already ordering lunch. I can see them, but not get down there.

That is when a couple of guys come up the hill in T-shirts and sunglasses, just to "look at the pass". When Hell freezes over, I imagine it is the far side of Thorong La. I hate the world. I just want to get back down on flat ground.

Two more hours. A zombie shuffle along the edge of the Mustang steppe, still going down, down to Muktinath, into the BOB MARLEY HOTEL ("Rasta Restaurant − Reggae Bar"). No dormitory tonight. Ten single rooms, please.

I wake up in the dark, alone. Stiff from cold and broken muscle, tense against the outside world. Late evening, according to the phone. Scrape together some damp clothes off the floor, mumble curses in the dark, fumble for a light switch. The BOB MARLEY Rasta Restaurant − Reggae Bar is empty. Skulk around the corridors, up and down the stairs in the little wooden atrium, without a plan. No idea where the others went. I sure hope they are sleeping behind these doors. I feel like a bear woken up mid-winter. There is no hot water in the shower. Teeth chattering.

The Fun Scale

Type I: activities that are simply fun while they happen.
Type II: activities that are fun only in retrospect after the worst parts have been forgotten, but make for good stories.
Type III: activities that are not fun, where the retelling never becomes rose-tinted.

The Annapurna Circuit itself is *Type I* fun, an I-can't-believe-this-is-real joy for weeks. Crossing Thorong La is definitely a *Type II* affair, a body-crushing but soul-lifting experience that I wanted to end, but that I will recommend and re-tell with hard-won fondness.

Standing in the cold shower, bent over in cramp, on trembling legs, trying to wipe away cold soap that won't lather, shaking and chattering from cooling down even more: *Type III* non-fun that I will never forget and never forgive.

Is this what the Tragic Bus to Pokhara prepared me for? If so, it worked.

Dinner: a stack of pizzas, watery beer and very little conversation. I leave the trekking poles that Thorong La bent, yanked apart and snapped, laying on the floor of my hotel room in Muktinath.

53

FORBIDDEN KINGDOM

MUKTINATH TO JOMSOM, NEPAL

The forbidden kingdom of Mustang, the Land of Lo, lies wedged between the Annapurnas and the Dhaulagiri massif, on the Gurung salt trade route between Tibet and Nepal. Mustang is dusty roads and hills billowing with ochre bushes and dry grass. Ruined sections of fortress walls totter to the sides of the path, perched on rocks wrinkled like curtains. Along the bottom of the valley lie green patchwork fields, but no tropical growth and no snow. There are a few villages below us, gathered around boxy monasteries on cliffs. The Dhaulagiri mountains blocks the monsoon so almost nothing grows on this arid ground, but more than a thousand years ago Tibetan traders connected it to the north over the mountain passes. Yak trains loaded with barley ran up through the Kali Gandaki valley, through the Mustang kingdom, over the Marang La mountain pass, and sold the grains into Tibet. They returned loaded with salt, distilled from lakes on the Tibetan high plateau. The Kingdom of Mustang thrived on the salt trade, and the small capital of Lo Mantang served as a commercial hub.

The forbidden kingdom of Mustang created a remote but stable monarchy behind the Himalayas: the current king is the direct descendant of a warrior who founded the kingdom in 1380, a lineage unbroken for more than 600 years. All the while the Habsburg monarchy, the Ming dynasty and the Aztec empire rose and fell, the Mustang hid up here. It was closed to outsiders for centuries, and only started issuing permits to enter in 1992.

We wander on rough roads through an unbroken monarchy in a Tibetan secret region, founded by warriors and hidden behind fortresses, embedded in a remote valley of the Nepalese Himalayas. Mustang is properly mythical.

Today, we hope to reach Jomsom, which we believe to be a proper city, but the landscape is wide and unchanging, so the map is not helping us to reckon how far we have to go. When dark clouds slosh up the valley, it is clear that we will be soaked for hours. We stop, gear up for rain, put on jackets and backpack covers, scarves and pull up hoods over our heads. At a particularly wrinkly patch of ground, we spy a jeep and an xtreme-sport production team preparing to shoot breakneck BMX bike stunts on the hills.

∽

THE RAIN DOES NOT COME. We climb down into the vivid village of Kagbeni and treat ourselves to a lunch of garlic-heavy yak burgers. Hey look, they have YacDonald's here!

The rain hits the moment we step outside again. We give up and follow the example of another group of trekkers: rent space in the back of decorated cargo trucks that make their way down the riverbed. It is crowded, uncomfortable and dark in the back of the truck; eight or ten people sitting on *stuff* and lying this way and that across each other's laps. Someone lifts the rubber tarp to let in some light and see what we are sitting on. Oh... gas canisters. That's great.

Within minutes, the truck in front of us blows a tire on the narrow road and blocks the entire convoy. Just as well. We hop off the gas canister death trap and continue on foot in the rain, out of Kagbeni and out of Mustang.

The last forbidden kingdom in history is now a lost kingdom. After the Nepalese civil war, when Nepal became a republic, Mustang lost its status as tributary kingdom. The last king is retired and when he goes, so goes the Kingdom of Mustang, the Land of Lo.

54

THE DOG ON POON HILL

JOMSOM TO GHOREPANI, NEPAL

One Team Europa member needs to break early and return to work; he needs to reach the airport in Pokhara earlier than we can make it on foot. No big deal, we will find a bus from Jomsom. But all buses are suspended due to a strike, and the military is here. Together with a stranded pair of volunteering sisters from Germany, we scour the small town for options. As small as Jomsom is, it is the transport hub for the region. No buses. The prices of jeeps carrying people down the gorge have risen to levels he can not afford. The trail south is the only road through the Kali Gandaki, which just happens to be the deepest valley in the world, so the selection of jeeps and buses will be the same further down the road.

The obvious solution is right outside the hotel window: the tarmac rectangle of Jomsom airfield. nepalcheapflights.com insists that "the flight from Jomsom to Pokhara is easy and is not risky [but] the flight is possible only in the morning because it gets windy in the afternoon".

Looking at that recommendation and at:

- the narrow air corridor between Dhaulagiri and Nilgiri peaks

- the Jomsom air crash that killed fifteen passengers two years ago
- the fact that the operating airline is banned from flying into the EU
- and that it seems to be pronounced "Terror Airlines"

...makes it an unattractive option. When do the buses resume service, do you think?

There is no departure schedule at Jomsom airport, only a weather report instead: the plane leaves soon, because there is "not much wind". Purchase an airplane ticket at a completely justifiable price: 25% of a normal bus ticket. It is strange to have the outside world reach into remote Mustang and pluck one of us out into the normal world. We breathlessly watch his tiny prop plane lift off, zip away between the cliffs before hooking a 90° turn down the Gandaki and out of sight.

After Jomsom, the trail follows the jeep road. Trucks and a few buses tear up great dust clouds, making the passage hard to appreciate. When dark rainclouds gather up to the north again, we swallow our pride: together with an Italian couple, we pool a lot of money and rent a jeep to take us a few villages down the road.

THE RIVERBED FALLS AWAY, and we cling to the narrow dirt track in a white jeep with hundreds of meters of free fall below. Long wire bridges hang free in the air, criss-crossing the vertical jungle valley.

The jeep is so close to the abyss that the road can't be seen through the windows. Those in the front seats can see the jeep hold to the middle of the road. I sit in the back and can only see the road we have survived. Cannot see even half-way down the gorge, only the thin grey line we have come down along and I try to not imagine how this road would look printed in a tabloid newspaper back home.

I try to come up with an excuse to get out and trek the last bit. Never been this scared. Denmark and Canada Jr. sit, bored, with their backs to the abyss, but I face it, teeth clenched so hard they could fracture, knuckles white. I can physically feel my noradrenaline glands draining; cortisol pouring out by the minute. Every little jolt, curve and bump is a dreadful mental image: the front left wheel missed the edge, gravel scrapes the jeep's undercarriage, and the rear wheels spin in a spray of gravel before…

I tell myself that people drive on these roads by the thousands every day without dying. Unfortunately, that is not true. Jeeps and buses fall off all the time.

But now I see the bottom of the valley, which is better than seeing only cliffs and landslides. When the Kali Gandaki gorge flattens and widens, the sky opens behind us again, diesel blue and heavy with thunder. I am suddenly thankful that we will not be trekking down when those clouds dump their water onto the gravel roads.

The jeep pulls into Tatopani in the afternoon, spilling us out at the bottom of a village that climbs the valley wall. Streets, staircases and ladders stacked between rows of gaudy houses. *Tato* = hot, *pani* = water, which is why we are stopping here: hot springs. Shallow cast concrete pools, searingly hot water, cold beer and there's even popcorn sold in a stall. Thunder stays behind us while the sun sets across the southern opening of the Kali Gandaki.

Canada Sr., the seasonal firefighter, cuts into me and Denmark talking: "Have you noticed that you use different voices when you speak to each other than when you speak English?" Yeah. I guess. We are giddy, all the way out here. A sense of Scandinavian fellowship rarely happens closer to home.

As night deepens into black, bats swoop low across the steaming water.

~

THE ROAD out of Tatopani goes across wood-and-rope bridges up the valley, and then leads up to Ghorepani at the foot of Poon Hill, the most famous lookout point in all of the Himalayas. It overlooks the entire Kali Gandaki with a perfect amphitheatre view of Annapurna to the right, and the Dhaulagiri to the left, all angled so sunrise lights up their peaks.

Getting there, however, is a nine-hour ascent up rough-cut stone stairs. Discard any ideas of limiting altitude changes: this is an altitude delta of 1600 meters in a single day, a single uphill battle. As lactic acid builds to a constant burn and the day gets hotter, Nature throws in a bonus: thinning out the oxygen supply again.

For all the pain, the ascent is beautiful. The southern peak of Nilgiri Himal vanishes behind us. We soar up through little villages with terraces, kitchen gardens, goat farms, swaying crop fields and schoolchildren bouncing up the stairs at twice my speed. Through a steep rhododendron forest, knotty trunks and leaves as thick as my hand, flowers so intensely pink they must be either artificial or early signs of a stroke.

A stroke? A hallucination? If they had not said hello first, I would have walked on and called it a misunderstanding off some sort. But hello! There they are: the French vagabond couple from Iran. Hello. How are you? Cool to see you here.

It is too weird; too unexpected. Over a month later, four countries later, three thousand kilometres away, in a village no more than a few houses along a staircase in rural Nepal. It is such a violation of coincidence that I do not know what to say. "This is crazy"? "Nice to meet you again"? "Bonne chance"? "This can not be happening"? Meeting them *again* is such a surprise that I am back on the stairs in just a couple of minutes.

But what was I supposed to say, really?

I have fallen far behind the others. Still have kilometres to go; hundreds of meters of pure altitude to eat.

> *"Life is not about*
> *how many breaths you took*
> *but the moments*
> *that took your breath away!"*

This must be AMAZING then, because I cannot breathe.

Canada Sr. snaps a picture of miserable me cresting the last few steps to a hotel in Ghorepani. I sit in the dining hall for half an hour mustering the strength to climb the final fifteen or so steps to where I have a thin mattress in a cell with walls of flimsy MDF board and windows from plastic sheeting. I have built carnival floats with more structural integrity than this, and dug out snow caves with better indoor heating.

Good thing I will not have to be cold for very long: we are leaving at 4AM to climb the last 400 meters to Poon Hill.

A sign proclaims World Happiness Day – "Inspiring you to be joyful!"

I refuse.

. . .

4.30AM. Out in the dark cobblestone street again. Fine mist. Dew. Muscles tense against the cold again. Another 400 meters of altitude to gain before sunrise. Better be worth it.

Together with a group of other trekkers we look for the way to Poon Hill, wandering in and out of alleys between the plywood houses before we find the gates and a stone-paved path winding up into a forest.

I am not feeling well after yesterday's climb. A strange, tingling migraine aura. Run down the altitude sickness symptom list. Headache? Yes. Dizzy? Kinda. Nausea? No. Fatigue? You think? Shortness of breath? For the past two weeks. Inability to walk: hell no. Let's say exhaustion, lack of sleep, thin air and... I am alone. I have lost the others again. Clip on the headlamp and push on up. The sky is already brightening in the east, but it is still pitch dark here under the trees.

Leaves rustle. There is something here; an animal in the bushes. Stand absolutely still. Click-click of claws on stone, pushing through bushes. Panting.

Is this:

1. a dangerous animal
2. onset of High Altitude Cerebral Edema hallucinations
3. a big, yellow friendly dog?

Luckily, it is door number three, a Retriever-looking mutt making its morning tail-wag round up to Poon Hill. An early riser, an entrepreneur, pawing its way up to where all the nice people go in the mornings.

At Poon Hill's summit, there is only biting morning air between us and the cathedral of Himalaya. It is everything they said it would be: some of the highest mountains in the world in a serrated line; a saw blade of ice curved around the horizon. The morning is so crystal clear that we can see the rough skin of Annapurna I, where Maurice Herzog clawed his way up the first recorded ascent of an 8000-meter peak. With a fatality rate at around 40%, Annapurna is the most dangerous of the eight-thousanders. For the first time I understand how unbelievably, impossibly large it is. Look at her. Just try to imagine how long a day's march along that ridge would be.

The sky brightens into a cornflower blue. We all sit in awe, slurping hot tea from steel mugs. Red sunlight hits the peaks and runs like honey down their sides. Lamjung Himal, Annapurna I, II, III, IV and the South peak; Machhapuchhre, Hiunchuli in front of them. Off to the west, the sun lights up Nilgiri, Tukuche and Dhaulagiri.

All the while, a yellow-furred whirlwind works the crowd for attention and affection, crawls under trekkers' arms to be held, puts a cold nose in our faces with big black eyes asking for biscuits.

55

INTO THICK AIR

GHOREPANI TO POKHARA, NEPAL

And then, finally, we are on the last leg of the trek, descending from the Poon Hill ridge down to Pokhara again. On the home side of Ghorepani, another stone staircase falls away into mist. Still early morning and the high jungle recedes into ghostly mist on both sides. As the day drags on, the sun boils the mist into damp and heavy air. The stairs wind between knotty trees and across little waterfalls, and my knees start popping.

Little villages line this path, and soon we start meeting groups of trekkers coming up this way, up to Poon Hill from the other end of the Circuit. More new faces than I have seen in weeks. The trekking high season has started while we were away. As difficult it is to come down the stairs on sore feet and weak knees under backpacks, the people going up must have a rough day. Hours and hours of continuous stair climbing in the baking heat, without two weeks of walking to prepare them.

Canada Sr. turns out to be the Great Satan himself, "comforting" those who climb up the stairs that they're "almost there," and that they "can rest around the bend". Their relieved and tired eyes light up. But no, they have hours of stairs left to climb.

There are more than 3000 stone stair steps below Ghorepani. 3000 shocks to the lower back, and as my legs weaken, it gets worse: sloppier steps, absorbing more shocks in the thighs, putting more into the muscles. Backpack straps start chafing.

On the other hand, we are descending back into normal air pressure. Drink deeply of oxygen. Baking heat after being chilled to the bone at Poon Hill's dawn. Crisp mountain air is exchanged for swirling spices and the smell of tilled earth. The peaks smell only of metal and ozone, while this end of the khola smells like a kitchens and gardens.

We crash out of the bamboo forest into the low point of the route at Birethanti. Take a silent lunch by a little brook. A donkey train cling-clang past down the stairs. We look at each other, nod, then march the last few kilometres to the final trekking station. Stamp our permits one last time, rent a jeep and roll down dusty roads to Pokhara.

It is strange to be back. Paved roads and people everywhere. We make dinner plans for the night and go our separate ways. I head back to the Celesty Inn, greeted by the chess-player. Call my parents. Blackout sleep in a warm room and a soft bed.

Wake up late in the afternoon to a deafening rainfall.

PART VI

KINNEKULLE TO KATHMANDU

As soon as I had learned to read on my own, I tore through the Tintin albums, over and over. I was taken in by the more mystic stories: Shooting Star, 7 Crystal Balls, Prisoners of the Sun and, naturally, Tintin in Tibet. The levitating lama, the remote monasteries, the promise of the Yeti...

And that one wide panel of Kathmandu streets. The temple's moss-covered roof, the red wood beams reaching for their roofs, the monkey and lion statues at the top of a few steps up from the streets. The monk with the umbrella. Bas reliefs above the windows.

It is time now. We are going into that panel. To Durbar Square, Kathmandu.

56

LAST LEG

POKHARA TO KATHMANDU, NEPAL

We stay another two days in Pokhara, in an orgy of pizza and burgers. Two members of Team Europa leave to go across that border at Sunauli into India; others hang out on the empty roof of the hotel. From up there you can see Machhapuchhre's fishtail held up high in the sky. It is strange to stand up here in neon lights and look back across the Gandaki zone, back into the Annapurnas.

My trip is coming to its end. I have sat cross-legged on the Celesty Inn bed with all my stuff spread out around me. It is not a lot. Bought the return ticket home from Kathmandu. Just a little QR code on my phone, and a 20-hour flight back. I wonder if there are things, people, contexts, routines back home that I can't remember now. If there is something important I can't think of.

RAINS WASH the streets of Pokhara. Buffalo block them. Scooters swerve around them. I wear flip-flop sandals now. My boots lie strewn on the hotel floor. I find my way back to the woman who sold me the trekking permit to let her know I have come back down from the trail again. We book a taxi to drive us to the bus station early in the morning. We take a final dinner and beers in the garden before splitting up Team Europa.

Tomorrow afternoon, a bus will roll into the capital and end this trip – Kinnekulle to Kathmandu. To lace the boots and shrug on the backpack again is an emotional déjà vu. We are back in a bus snaking down serpentine roads again. The smell of tropic jungle and petrol grows stronger as we trundle toward Kathmandu. The long, narrow coils of road carry caravans of buses and trucks, above, far below, across the valley, ahead and behind. It is a bewildering tangle, a steep tangle, a tangle with chasms on one side and steep dirt on the other. Brake drums squeak for hours on end.

We pass a water fountain with a message spray-painted on its side: WRONG WAY. But it is not the wrong way.

Hey, Kathmandu. I have made it here. Rust-red, earthen, ochred, dusty. We sneak out early after dawn and catch sunrise warming brick walls, creeping along narrow alleys and backyards. We find tiny shrines belonging to a specific apartment block, metal Buddhas smeared with purple. We find bicycles chained to basketball hoops, black streaks of shoe rubber underneath. We find low doors and arches leading into labyrinths. Once morning has come, we pull up chairs outside a café and take breakfast. We head into touristy Thamel and read Sharpie wall scribbles in from a pile of pillows. *Life is a party! Have fun! Breathe in! Smile out! Nature makes us feel grateful for the beautiful gift of life! NEPAL = Never-Ending Peace And Love! You are the Universe and the Universe is You!*

We circle the Boudhanath stupa clockwise under its stern gaze and settle into a lazy flow between houses, streets, gardens, restaurants, alleys and then settle back on our roof. Thunder comes back in the evening: violet lightning on yellow sky, light drizzle on the tarp. Bad weather comes up from the Kathmandu valley.

Kathmandu's power grid comes and goes, and tonight it goes. In our rooms, the evening runs slowly in a dim glow of battery-powered e-books while the rain hammers the window. Faint blinks of distant lightning. Wales and Canada Sr. leave for Myanmar tomorrow. Italy and Canada Jr. stay in KTM without plans. I am going home.

After dark, we duck through a low door, through a room of heavy wood furniture and dark tables. Round a corner to a short corridor. Climb narrow little staircases and ladders, duck under roof beams and push open a door. Dinner and thunder on a roof illuminated by yellow neon lights, hidden behind a shifty tattoo parlour on Old Freak Street.

The Hippie Trail used to end here. Still does, I guess. Freak Street was the grounding connection for the hippie current from the west. All the way from London, through Turkey and past the signboard in the Pudding Shop, Iran and through ancient Persepolis, Afghanistan and through the Khyber Pass, Pakistan and onto the Grand Trunk Road, India and past the *ghats* in Varanasi, into Nepal to finally run up here, on Old Freak Street. Last stop for the Intrepids. Just a stone's throw up the street is Durbar Square, where dark-red brick temples from the 12th century sit covered in grey city doves. I try to take in that I made it here; that my Hippie Trail ran up here according to plan. Up here, to the ancient temples of Durbar Square.

I've made it to the end. Clink two empty beer bottles together. Hey. Simmer down, will you? I would like to say something.

57

PROCEED THROUGH SECURITY

KATHMANDU, NEPAL

Alright, safe travels! Three of us plop into a taxi that swerves away from Italy and Canada Jr. and into gridlocked traffic toward Tribhuvan Airport. Wales' and Canada's plane to Thailand and Myanmar leaves in a couple of hours. My plane leaves later tonight, well after dark. About time.

> ...be kind to those who welcome you. They have been expecting my old self and are a little afraid that this is not the person who has arrived. Their world did not move in the short time that I have been gone forever. There was no rift in reality here; nothing occurred that did not already have a name.
>
> — After the Adventure, Morgan Hite

This trip has been in the back of my head in different versions for a very long time. The idea to sit by a river in India came from a radio show. Going to Iran by train came from looking up how far you can go on an Interrail pass. Pakistan from came a weird Youtube clip. The Himalayas came from Tintin, I suppose. Going overland came from a forum post. To backpack for months came from an opportunity after school. It is a big thing to have checked all of them off the list. But I'm still me. I was here all along.

Perhaps there will be a sort of clarity after this. Or perhaps I will be insufferable: *I don't think you understand, when I travelled to Nepal...*

I am jolted out of this reflection by Canada and Wales. They have checked their bags and are heading through security. Meet you upstairs? Yeah, sure, I'll be up in a minute.

That is the last I see of them. My check-in gate doesn't open for another five hours, so I can't go through security until tonight. So, after weeks of spending every waking hour together, after cresting Thorong La, after the jeep ride down to Tatopani, after sunrise at Poon Hill – that was it. "Yeah, sure, I'll be up in a minute".

They say solo travelling is not lonely, that you leave on your own, but you are never alone on the road. From the train to Denmark to the taxi to Kathmandu's airport, that has been true. But now, in the last few hours, it is just me on a plastic chair in the Kathmandu departure hall for five hours.

58

CLOSER THAN IT APPEARS

KATHMANDU TO HOME, SWEDEN

The yellow dots on the runway tilt away as the plane climbs out of Kathmandu valley. The sky is clear; white stars hang all around us.

There is a strange asymmetry in going away slowly for months and popping back home in a matter of hours. I stare at the back of the seat in front me; try to savour this moment of completion, of returning, of going home, putting these checkmarks on the bucket list. I stare out at the night where there is nothing but blackness and a lantern at the wingtip. Try to feel wistful, sentimental, reluctant to go back to the cage. But I am just exhausted. Looking forward to being home again.

I scroll through the music in my phone. Months ago, I selected this track to be the soundtrack to turning back around. It was supposed to be profound, a fittingly melancholic piano trill building to a steady rhythm: *What do you go home to?* by Explosions in the Sky. But I sit just behind the wing so the song is drowned out by the engines, and I realise the album title is more fitting than the song name anyway: *All of a sudden I miss everyone.*

Maybe there is no point in making a big deal out of this.

Maybe it is not possible to wring profundity or poignancy out of 28 hours on plastic chairs and in airplane seats.

Maybe I am trying too hard.

There is one thing I have learned.

Well, not learned, but *verified*: this advertisement sticker that I saw years ago on a shop window. For all the finding of the self that did or did not happen, this is true:

ACKNOWLEDGMENTS

Dear mother, dear father; somehow more eager than terrified. Thank you for all that led from Denmark ferries to this.

Nina; thank you for your enthusiasm in wrapping the .pdf in art.

Shah Cheragh photo provided by Maryam Norozi.
Wagah Border ceremony screenshot by Shahid Shafqat.

READING

Across Asia on the Cheap. Lonely Planet. (1973)
After the Adventure. Morgan Hite. (1990)
A ride to India across Persia and Baluchistán. Harry de Windt (1891)
G. and Co's Overland Circular. (1854)
Historical Library. Diodorus. (c:a 60 BCE)
Kim. Rudyard Kipling. (1901)
Magic Bus. Rory MacLean. (2006)
Road to Oxiana. Robert Byron. (1937)
Thomas Was Alone. Mike Bithell. (2010)
The Overland Companion: Being a guide for the traveller to India via Egypt. J. H. Stocqueler. (1850)
The Pakistan Chronicles. Adam Hodge. (2012)
Paleofuture: What International Air Travel Was Like in the 1930s. Matt Novak. (2013)

CPSIA information can be obtained
at www.ICGtesting.com
Printed in the USA
LVHW110219050123
736521LV00004B/147